AF486820

Code Pink

Marilyn Ludwig

For Debbi Daniel-Wayman and the Fair Isle Book Store
Washington Island, Wisconsin

For my friend, Linda Surlak,
who has been waiting a long time for this one.

And for all searching for home.

Marilyn signing books at Debbi's Fair Isle Book Store,

I may not have gone where I intended to go,
but I think I have ended up where I needed to be.
—Douglas Adams

Chapter One

"I'M AN OLD WIDOW AND a compulsive chatterbox," she said blithely, settling back as comfortably as possible for one attached to many tubes. Felicity Sinclair, called Flick by some, continued her monologue. "I'm as wilted as leftover lettuce salad." She sighed. "Especially now. My friend Carmel is my opposite — an ultra-serious scientist — a pharmacist, actually. Single, of course, and terribly, terribly earnest. I don't think she's ever been in a relationship. Never married and doesn't want to be. She's very good looking, you know, in a business-like way. Proper, wearing the kind of pants we used to call slacks, dark short hair in a pixie cut. Not dumpy and puffy, like me. You could search from coast to coast and never find two friends more different. It's not just our ages — I'm much older — it's temperament, background, everything."

Felicity carried on, trying to ignore the elastic stretched too tightly on her wrist and arm, keeping the wires in place. "But we are best friends — best I've ever had, anyway. She is the only one who still calls me by my childhood nickname, Flick. My father used it to dismiss me. Then my husband carried on the tradition, which is why I relegated the name to the past — until Carm came along. Ralph — that was my husband — used to say 'Flick off,' when he was mad, and even during the odd times he wasn't. I suppose it was funny, but it never appealed to my sense of humor. Ah, well, we were talking about Carm. We're best friends, so it's okay to tease each other. I say to her, 'First do no harm, Carm,' and then she says —"

Felicity was on a roll—enjoying herself thoroughly—when she was interrupted by a rude, eardrum-breaking blast.

ALERT!

CODE PINK! CODE PINK!

ALERT! CODE PINK!

TO YOUR STATIONS! CODE PINK!

The urgent message, filling not only the room but also the entire hospital, ended Felicity's determined monologue. Under different circumstances, the nurse might have been relieved to escape the role of captive listener, for it was apparent Felicity planned to continue the saga of the amazing Carm.

"I'll be back as soon as I can," said the nurse, whose nametag read Shirley. "You hold on tight, dearie."

How annoying to be interrupted when she and Shirley were enjoying each other's company.

Felicity could tell Shirley was rattled by the alert, but not nearly as much as her aide, a striking young woman with a gorgeous name that did justice to her appearance. Selena froze, and for a brief moment her dark eyes met Felicity's faded hazel. Then she, too, fled. That was unfortunate. Felicity had been hoping to talk privately with her once Shirley left. Perhaps alone, Selena would stop being shy and become an interesting companion. But now everyone was gone because of the mysterious *Code Pink*.

Felicity tried to reach the persistent itch on her back she'd been able to ignore as long as she had an audience. She might be more tolerant of her discomfort if she knew what the alert was about. Guess it had to be serious for Shirley to rush out just as she was about to detach her from all these gadgets.

Code Pink. Hospitals seemed to be full of codes. *Code Blue* was the only one Felicity had heard of before. That meant the patient wasn't breathing or his heart had stopped—she wasn't quite sure which. But it did mean someone was going to die unless someone else did something fast. "Maybe *Code Blue* is for men and *Code Pink* for women," Felicity said out loud, needing to fill the silence with a voice, even if it were her own. "Sexist in this day and age, but at least it makes sense."

Not being able to breathe. That's what had brought her here. What started off as a cold—"Code: in the Node," she scribbled quickly into her notebook, hoping to turn it into a humorous poem someday—ended with the nasty, relentless case of bronchitis that resulted in her first experience in a hospital bed. Well, not the only time she should have been, but the first time she actually ended up there. And then, once she was finally in the hospital, she came down with double pneumonia. Dear Carm had been pretty certain she was going to die. Felicity wondered if it would have been a great loss if she had. "Nonsense!" she said, trying to quiet the inner voice that always tried to knock her down.

This bed was comfortable, even if the tubes and adhesive holding everything in place weren't. Everyone should be issued a hospital bed to take home. She giggled at the thought. Carmel had been right to bring her here, even though she had protested at the time.

Code Pink surely caused the floor to empty in a hurry. "Swish!" she said, describing the sound the nurses made as they'd rushed through the halls. "Bang!" she described the quick closing of doors. Felicity had never trusted silence—too often in her life it had been followed by violence—and now, suddenly, the hall seemed hollow. All those needing help nearby were clearly out of luck. Too bad she'd finished all the *Times* puzzles for the day. They had become too easy. With a great sigh, she turned on the television, even though she'd prefer live people for company.

The large clock next to the TV proclaimed the time as two o'clock. Two in the afternoon, which didn't feel right exactly. Felicity was getting her days and nights mixed up. For two weeks, if not sleeping, she had been hooked up to a breathing device, or having her temperature taken, or blood pressure checked. No one stays in the hospital this long anymore, she thought. Maybe Carm's grim diagnosis was correct. Maybe she had been at death's door. Carm would have been sad if she had died, but no one else would have cared. And no one anywhere would have received a sympathy card—"Sorry for your loss, but she's gone to a better place"—or a tuna, noodles, and peas casserole.

At least Carm would arrive soon with interesting tales of her forlorn teenage niece and the monster dog from hell. Carm should never have agreed to take care of them while her brother and his wife went vagabonding in Switzerland. What were they doing there? Mountain climbing? Yodeling? Eating chocolates? And why they would go to Switzerland with her brother sick? It was so incomprehensible Carm must be keeping something from her. Poor Carm! The niece was challenging enough, but the dog—well, actually, Carm seemed to prefer the dog to the niece. Felicity supposed it wouldn't be so bad if the dog were a tiny little thing, but—

"Flick, I'd like you to meet Alfred," Carmel had said, showing her a photo of the largest beast Felicity had seen since—*no, don't go there*—well, since gazing through bars in a zoo. In the photo, Alfred seemed to be smiling—friendly enough, just oversized.

At the time, though, Felicity wasn't prepared to think of anything but herself. She'd handed the photo back. "Alfred? Odd name, isn't it?"

"King Alfred, the Great Dane," Carm replied. "Fits him perfectly, don't you think?"

"Not really, when you consider that King Alfred ended the Danish conquests."

"Oh, you . . . " Carm had snorted. "Too much History Channel again. And what would you name him, Flick?" Felicity had no idea and was grateful it wasn't her problem.

Code Pink was taking a long time to end, but she wouldn't complain. Even after Ralph died, Felicity continued to portray a happy, positive disposition, as befitting her name—a half-full kind of gal. Patience had always been her forte, possibly her salvation. But she was longing to be done with all these wires and gadgets and that painful tape on her wrist and arm. Perversely, she now had to go to the bathroom—probably just because she couldn't. No, the blame must be shared with the fluid that had been pumping into her for more hours than she could count.

She would be as patient as a saint. Even Ralph would have been proud of her. No, her imagination couldn't extend that far. Needing to pee was not a crisis. Somewhere in this hospital, someone was in real trouble. Felicity was safe, although uncomfortable, and would go home soon—maybe tomorrow.

This whole hospital experience could prove to be an interesting adventure, and she had a whole notebook of possible poems that might come from it. "Code Pink," she wrote underneath "Death's Door." Should it be a funny or serious poem? Or maybe she should think big. A hospital thriller novel? No, she was finished with all things scary. A collection of simple but humorous poems would do.

"What in the name of God is going on here?"

Felicity grimaced. Speaking of scary—that obnoxious woman again! At least all the rooms on this floor were singles. It could be entertaining to have a roommate, but what if it were that woman or someone like her? Loud, brassy, everyone in the hall could hear her complaints, and that weasel of a husband who came to visit was more obnoxious than—well, Ralph! But it seemed that Mr. Usher was on the hospital board, so the nurses waited on his wife hand and foot. Felicity could tell how the nurses felt by their exasperated expressions whenever they were in Felicity's room and the woman pressed her finger on the buzzer. Selena, especially, seemed dismayed and fearful. The others were just annoyed. "Yes, Your Majesty! Right away, Mrs. Usher," Nurse Shirley always said.

A title came to mind, even though it had been used before. She wrote it down—*The Fall of the House of Usher*. No, she'd change it to *The Fall of Usher's Hospital*. She was good at titles. One of her notebooks was filled with them. She'd write a parody of Poe. *A Parody of Poe*—another great title!

The voice in the hall reached the upper octaves. "Have you any idea why this entire hall is totally deserted, and no one can get help? I'm sure someone will die before anyone raises a finger. And then they won't care; they'll do a grand cover-up. You mark my words!"

Oh, dear. Felicity abandoned her potential poem and muted the TV. In a raging fury, the woman wheeled herself into the room. Suddenly, silence was preferable. "I'm sure it must be an emergency, Mrs. Usher, although I don't know what *Code Pink* means."

The woman glared at her. "How do you know my name? Are you one of those spies that seem to frequent this place? It's loaded with them, you know—illegal, dangerous aliens, all magically protected."

Aliens? Mrs. Usher was in the wrong ward for sure. Instead of encouraging her to take the elevator two floors up where she clearly belonged, Felicity said instead, "Uh, I'm sorry, but the walls are thin, and my hearing is acute. Sometimes I hear conversations in other rooms when they're too loud." There! That was as confrontational as ever-cheerful Felicity permitted herself to be.

"Well, I'm sure I'm no louder than anyone else, under the circumstances. I don't know what *Code Pink* means, either. It sounds like a bit of fluff to encourage incompetence. I shall report this to my husband at once! He is on the hospital board, you know, and has very important connections with the government. He and our mayor are practically best friends."

Felicity said nothing. She didn't even allow herself a negative expression. Mrs. Usher seemed to find satisfaction, though, in giving her a dirty look before wheeling on to the next helpless victim.

Shaking her head, worrying slightly about whether the next poor soul's health could sustain an Usher invasion, Felicity returned to her notebook. "It's no use," she muttered, too uncomfortable to attempt even the weakest of poems. "I haven't wet the bed since I was four, but it's going to happen soon unless the mysterious alert ends." She clenched her teeth and tried not to think about it.

She would stay positive. After all, it was a pleasant room— sparkling clean, a large picture window with a fine view of the grounds of the hospital. Even a cushioned window seat, had she been allowed to sit there instead of being held prisoner in this suddenly too-narrow bed that had seemed perfectly fine a few minutes before. If this were a hotel, she would simply relax and go to the bathroom whenever she pleased. Well, she really must get up. Perhaps the contraption on wheels would come with her. But as soon as her feet reached the floor, an unholy alarm went off. Quickly, she retreated, but it was too late. What had she done? Was it legal? Felicity had always obeyed the law. How could she turn off the blasted thing? She pressed the button for the nurse, but it was useless. No one would come to her rescue. She'd almost prefer Mrs. Usher's rage to the sound of the buzzer, a different kind of alarm.

Could she detach everything herself? She stared at the wires connecting her with several unknown machines and the bandages on her arm. They were too tightly wrapped and were starting to itch. A bag of fluid continued to pour something into her body. At least she no longer was attached to the mechanism that had rid her of the awful phlegm that had prevented her from breathing. But now that she was almost better, she was still terribly uncomfortable and trapped.

Then she felt warmth spreading throughout the bed sheets. Too late. Felicity blushed. Not her fault, but still . . . So embarrassing, and there was no possible way for her to hide it.

ATTENTION! ATTENTION!
CODE PINK CANCELLED. ONLY A TEST!
REPEAT: ONLY A TEST!
Staff, you are to be congratulated.
You may return to your duties.
Patients, thank you for your patience!"

"Patients, thank you for your patience?" They could use some writing assistance. Or maybe it was a joke. Felicity shrugged. At least she had heard the announcement in spite of the obnoxious buzzer.

Finally, Nurse Shirley came to her rescue, turning off the alarm. "Don't you worry, Mrs. Sinclair. That will happen when you try to get out of bed. Now, let's get rid of all these pesky attachments, so you can go to the bathroom."

"It's too late, I'm afraid. I am sorry, but all the fluids . . ." Felicity blushed again.

Shirley smiled. "That happens. I'm sure you'd like the opportunity to clean up. Selena?" She turned to the aide. "Selena will help you while I see to my other patients. Now, don't worry about anything, Mrs. Sinclair."

No wonder Shirley smiled. She didn't have to do the dirty work.

Selena helped her out of bed, and, surprisingly, Felicity found that she did need assistance. Her first reaction after being down so long was dizziness. "Thank you. I am sorry, but everyone was gone for so long. Please tell me, what's a Code Pink?"

The young aide shook her head. "I don't understand," she said softly, but her eyes widened before her face became a complete blank.

The heck you don't. You might not speak much English, but you understand it well enough. I'll bet you don't miss a trick.

When Felicity returned from the bathroom, somewhat scrubbed and wearing a fresh hospital gown, her bed had clean linens. Selena was still in the room but a new nurse—Nurse Becky—had arrived to take Felicity's blood pressure, temperature, and all those curious things medical people liked to do. Then she studied her watch.

"There you are," she said, in a cold, efficient manner. "Blood pressure and temperature normal, breathing normally."

"Thank you. Yes, I am relieved. I'm almost back to my old self. But do you know how long—"

"That will be the doctor's decision." Becky rushed out of the room.

"Huffy, huffy." It didn't matter that Selena was listening. "Surely anyone with the name Becky should be upbeat and cheerful. Well, I know my place, and I'll bet you do, too, Selena." Felicity received a grinning response from Selena before she, too, left the room.

"I wonder when Carm will come. Maybe problems with the kid and the dog." Felicity tried to work on her Code Pink poem. But without knowing what it meant, it was hard to proceed. Should the poem rhyme? Pink, blink, stink, ink, kink, drink, link, wink, preshrink, rethink . . . Maybe she should rethink writing it at all, or stick to blank verse. She closed her eyes.

The phone startled her from a dark, disturbing dream in which her ungrieved-for husband was calling her. When she was conscious, Felicity worked hard not to think of him. Ralph belonged to nighttime terrors and a different Felicity, one she hadn't been for three years. The phone . . . she grabbed it in time. "Hello . . . "

"At last!" a voice scolded. But that was just Carmel, who often sounded as if she were scolding—at least when addressing Felicity. Yes, they were best friends, but the younger woman was in charge.

"Carm, I was asleep. Are you still planning to come?"

"I did already, but the doors were locked, and no one answered the phone at the registration desk. Finally I went back home. What's going on?"

"Nothing now, but before we had something called Code Pink."

"Code Pink! Oh, my!"

Right. Carm knew a lot about hospitals and such. "It turned out to be a drill, but what's Code Pink?"

"Child abduction," Carm said. "That explains the locked doors. Extremely stressful for the staff. All the entrances and exits must be secured and every empty room searched. Good thing it was only a drill. Must have been pretty crazy, though."

"Crazy and stressful for me, too." Felicity giggled. "I wet the bed."

"Only you, Flick. Only you."

She was kidding, of course, but there was an edge to her voice Felicity did not appreciate. "First do no harm, Carm," she said, managing to get a slight edge into her voice, too. Sometimes Carmel had a way of making her feel small and foolish.

There was a pause, and then—"I'm sorry, Flick. That didn't come out right. I know you couldn't help it; it could happen to anyone."

"Okay," Felicity said.

"Look, there's some stuff going on right now—about my brother and his wife and about Natalie—"

"And the dog," Felicity finished.

"Well, yeah. The thing is I couldn't tell you about it when you were so sick, and—"

"And now you'll have to wait even longer," Felicity interrupted, as the doctor entered the room. "I'll get off right now, Dr. Elliott."

"Got it," Carm said. "Call me when you can."

Felicity's conversation with Dr. Elliott was delightful, of course, especially when he pronounced her fit as a fiddle. "Home sometime tomorrow," he promised. "Be sure to follow up with me next week and get lots of rest. You do not want a relapse this winter."

No, she truly didn't, Felicity reflected, once the doctor had left her alone, even though the encounters with various people here were quite pleasant. She winced at the sound of bellowing in the next room. At least most people were pleasant. Now that she was no longer hooked to her bed she would reap the benefits of this lovely place. Grabbing the current newspaper, she curled up on the window seat and gazed out at the quickly turning leaves. *Summer is over, and* fall has come. She opened her notebook and wrote the thought down. "Summer is over and fall has come." A good opening line for something. Perhaps autumn would sound more poetic.

But her happy thoughts vanished as she returned to the newspaper. Her eyes filled with tears of sorrow and rage. And that's how Selena found her as she wheeled the dinner cart into the room.

"Señora, what is wrong?"

"This!" Felicity pointed to a newspaper photo of a small boy with dark, frightened eyes and lips that seemed to be quivering. "He was taken from his parents at the border. He's only two. What's going to happen to him? How can he ever be normal and happy? Children! Babies! So many have been taken from their parents. All they want is to be a family with a safe place to live. The parents might never see their children again. And we're doing it now—in 2019. We're responsible!"

Selena nodded her head sadly. "But not you, Señora."

"Well, not me, personally, but what am I doing to stop it? Even here in our town it's happening. When neighbors disappear on streets near where I live, what do I do? Nothing! 'What happened to the Hernandez family?' people say, and no one knows. Whole families, who have lived here most of their lives, deported to dangerous places where they've never been. It's wrong!"

"Si, Señora Sinclair."

"Call me Felicity. It's friendlier. Selena, as soon as I get home, I'm going to find some way to help. Donate money. Something. Even a useless old lady like me should be able to do something."

"Will you be going home soon, Señora?"

"Tomorrow, Selena—to a lovely home, the largest one on Stratton Court—a great brown one with white trim, in the historic district—and unlike other parts of town, absolutely safe. I am so fortunate I don't even lock the door; I lost my key years ago. My husband was furious with me, but then he was most of the time, anyway. Truthfully, I am a much happier person without him, although I am grateful he left me well provided for. Listen to me chattering away again. Carm is always on me for that. She calls me a Flickful magpie. I imagine you don't understand half of what I'm saying, but I'm sure you agree with me about the poor children."

Selena smiled. "You will go home tomorrow to the big brown house on Stratton Court. Then you will do what you can to help. Eat now. I will return for your tray." Seemingly resolved to do something, Selena rushed out of the room.

Ha! Selena could speak more English than she let on. Now Felicity would enjoy this excellent meal. She couldn't understand why hospital food had such a poor reputation. Broasted chicken, mashed potatoes, peas—she wondered what was for dessert.

Later in bed, just as she turned out the light, Felicity remembered that she was supposed to call Carm. Something had been troubling her friend. Probably the dog pooped in the house, Felicity thought, before drifting off to sleep.

URR
Code Pink
Selene to Ariadne
Plan formed. Proceed.

CHAPTER TWO

CARMEL ABBOTT WONDERED BRIEFLY WHY Flick hadn't returned her call the day before but decided to be grateful for the silence. She looked worryingly at the spare room door that had been slammed shut only moments before. Charles's death, although difficult to accept, was at least planned and inevitable. But his nasty wife and heartbroken daughter were another thing altogether. Katy's rejection of her stepdaughter was totally unexpected. Carm never planned on dealing with an unhappy teenager, but King Alfred was a pleasant bonus. Carm liked dogs.

So far, your life has been a piece of cake, she told herself sternly. Up until now, no family crises that were your concern have come along, and at least you have a job with a kind boss, who allowed you to take a long leave of absence to deal with this. "It's a knotty situation," Bill had said, "but if anyone can handle it, you can. We will struggle along without you; don't give us a thought." He gave her an understanding grin, letting her know she'd be missed.

Loud sobs interrupted her thoughts, causing her to leave the couch and knock firmly on the door. "Natalie, please come out or let me in. It's okay if you don't go to school for a while."

"I'm never going back to school. You can't make me! I'll quit. I'm old enough. Then I'll get a job and an apartment and—" Natalie began to wail again, tears joined by hiccups. "No one wants me anyway."

Carm couldn't argue with that. Natalie's words were the truth. Carm wished she could say, "I want you," but she couldn't. Nat's only aunt didn't want her, and her stepmother didn't either. There was no one else. Carm opened her mouth to say something, but two phones rang: her own and Natalie's cell in the bedroom.

"Carm," trilled a happy voice. "You can come get me. I'm free at last!"

"What!" screamed a furious voice. "Where do you expect me to go? What about money? What about school? What about my things?" A pause. "Well, fine. I'll figure it out myself. You know what, Katy? I really hate you!" The door opened, and the formerly belligerent teen, now a childish mess of tears and tangled hair, threw herself into Carm's arms. "Aunt Carmel, what should I do? No one wants me?"

"Carm," the voice on her phone called out, "is something wrong? When can you get me?"

Holding Natalie tight, Carm tried to answer. "Flick, we've got some problems here. Either I or someone else will come as soon as possible. You hold tight."

"But—"

"But I've got to go, Flick." Carm wanted to add, "Please understand," but it was doubtful Flick would. She had been too ill to confide in before when the only goal was to keep her alive. Besides, Flick had a heart of gold, but she seldom really listened. With her arm around the shaking teenage child, Carm led her to the couch, where she handed her a box of tissues.

"Nat, I know your situation is bad, and I'll do whatever I can to make it better, but you have to talk to me."

Choking, barely able to get the words out, Natalie tried. "I knew Dad was going to die. It was hard, but I sort of accepted it, although I thought I should have gone with them to Switzerland. But Katy said no, and Dad did whatever she wanted. But I thought Katy would come back, and we'd live together, even if we don't like each other much."

Natalie started to cry again. Carm waited. "Take your time," she said, trying to stay calm as the phone began to ring again. Probably Flick, but she was safe and would have to wait. "What did Katy say, dear?"

"She said she's going to stay in Europe awhile to deal with her sorrow. She said that you're my blood relative, and you can figure out what to do with me. She's going to sell our home and said I should go take anything that's mine."

That unfeeling monster of a woman, Carm thought. Charles must have been out of his mind to marry her. But then, he was, when Natalie's mother died and shortly after he was diagnosed with lung cancer. Katy, who saw a short-term marriage and dollar signs, allowed Charles to cling to her like a raft.

"I don't think Katy can do that legally," Carm said. "We'll check with a lawyer. And she can't expect a barely seventeen-year-old to travel back and forth to New Mexico. The two of us will handle this together. At least you still have the most important thing."

Natalie attempted a wet smile. "You mean King Alfred?"

"King Alfred the Great. I'll see if he needs to go outside while you wash up. Then I'm afraid we have to go over to the hospital and spring my friend Felicity."

"But—"

"No buts. You're coming with me. Flick needs to be home. She's a dear friend, and she nearly died. She doesn't know what's going on here. You're not the only one who needs support. I do, too. And for the two of us to accomplish anything about your future, we need to know each other and become friends."

Natalie nodded. What choice did she have?

⬥

They were quiet in the car. Nat stared out the window at the burnt orange and red falling leaves. Autumn in Illinois was not like what she was used to in southern New Mexico. Aunt Carm's townhouse was small, hardly enough room for the two of them—never mind including Alfred. It was completely different from Dad's spacious adobe home with acres of land for Al to roam. But her aunt might not be so bad. At least she hadn't thrown her out—at least she liked Nat's dog. Nat would do her best to get along.

Obediently, she followed Carm to the second floor of the hospital. "Wait here," her aunt said, pointing to the lounge. "I'll make sure Flick is dressed and has signed everything."

Alone, Natalie thumbed through a few dated magazines. Pity she had been too upset to remember her cell phone. A pretty young woman peeked into the room. "*Hola*," she said. "I mean, hello. I did not know you were here. Are you well?"

Nat grinned. The woman's English was probably not as good as Natalie's Spanish. "*Aqui estamos*," she replied, continuing to speak in Spanish. "I'm waiting for my aunt. We're taking her friend, Mrs. Sinclair, home."

"Ah, *si. Una buena mujer*. And you speak Spanish?"

"*Si, hablo espanol.*"

The woman smiled, nodded, and disappeared.

Nat gave up on magazines and gazed out the window, a different world from what she'd seen so far. It looked like country out there. You would never think the hospital was close to downtown Aurora, the second largest city in Illinois. Then, to Nat's surprise, she saw the young Latina woman again, rushing to the parking lot, carrying a bundle—a bundle that looked like a baby. That was funny. Nat had assumed the woman was a hospital worker, instead of a mom taking her newborn home. Hadn't she indicated she knew Aunt Carm's friend? Odd, too, that she was alone. Natalie shrugged and continued to wait.

◆

Felicity thanked everyone who had taken care of her, especially the nurses, who wished her well and seemed sorry she was leaving. They didn't often have a patient so cheerful and accommodating, although it was likely they would have more time for other duties once she was gone. "I did want to say goodbye to Selena, though. Where is she, do you know?"

Nurse Shirley shook her head. "I saw her before. Maybe she is on break. I'll let her know you were asking about her."

"Never mind," Felicity said. "I'll come back for a visit. She had a *chalupa* recipe I was anxious to try." Not true, but Felicity felt she needed an excuse.

"Please hurry, Flick," Carm urged. "Nat's in the lounge waiting for us. She's been there quite awhile."

Felicity shrugged. "If what I've heard about teenagers is correct, she's busily texting all her friends. But very well, we can go — as soon as my chariot arrives."

"I'll check on your wheelchair again," Shirley said, before hurriedly leaving the room. "I believe Selena sent for it some time ago. I'll check on your niece, too, Miss Abbott. Mrs. Sinclair is probably correct about the cell phone."

Carm didn't bother to explain that her niece was currently friendless and hadn't brought her phone to the hospital — that all she had for entertainment were outdated magazines that wouldn't have amused her even if current.

"Oh, here it is! At long last!" Felicity announced, as an orderly wheeled in the chair. "Now for home! Won't it be wonderful? Let's go, Carm! What are you waiting for?"

Tired of the interminable wait, Natalie stood outside the door. "Oh, good," she said, when the door opened. "I was worried."

"Just taking my time saying goodbye to friends," Felicity said. "You must be Natalie."

Natalie nodded, uncertain what to say to something so obvious.

"And how is your dear father?"

"Dead." Natalie started toward the elevator, ahead of her aunt and the flighty woman in the wheelchair.

Felicity glared at Carmel. "You should have told me," she said.

Carm smiled sadly. "I know, but you were so sick, and then there never seemed to be a good time."

"And you could never get a word in edgewise. We'd better get caught up soon so I don't keep putting my foot in my mouth. But I am sorry about your brother, dear. Truly."

Carm nodded. "I'll carry your things and put them just inside your door, Flick. Will you be okay after that? Nat and I have been away longer than I expected, and we need to get home to King Alfred."

"Before he tears up the furniture, I imagine. You have your hands full. I'll be fine, dear."

———◆———

"So what do you think of my friend?" Carmel asked, as they pulled out of Felicity's driveway.

Nat squirmed. Truthfully, she didn't think much of the elderly woman, but she was stuck with Aunt Carm—for now. She would choose her words wisely. "She's awfully pretty for an old lady and seems nice enough. She talks a lot, doesn't she?"

Carmel laughed. "She does indeed—practically nonstop—and I'm never quite sure what she hears." Carm stopped to think before continuing. "Try not to judge her, Nat." She grinned. "That's my job, and I'm afraid I do it often and too thoroughly. Look, I'm going to tell you a few things I probably shouldn't, but since you're going to be around for the foreseeable future—Well, you probably should know about Flick and how we met. Starting about five years ago when I first got my job, she used to come into the pharmacy often, with one injury after another. She didn't come to fill prescriptions, although she bought plenty of over-the-counter pain pills. No, she bought bandages and ice bags and ointments for her bruises."

"I guess I see where this is going," Nat said.

"Probably." Teenagers today catch on fast, she thought. Maybe too fast. "Well, in time, I could see where it was going, too. Several years ago—must be over three now—I insisted that she have a cup of tea with me back in the office. There, finally, she admitted that her husband abused her, physically and mentally, but that she was afraid to leave him." At Nat's look, Carm continued. "Yeah, I know, a typical story, but not typical for the person suffering. Ralph was wealthy and controlled all the money, doling out pitiful amounts occasionally to Flick. And he rarely allowed her to speak above a whisper. Their house was like a funeral home."

"She speaks plenty now," Nat observed.

"Indeed. An overreaction, I think. Flick became terrified of silence, because of the anger that often followed. That's why she keeps on chattering. Well, in a strange way, we became friends and shared many cups of tea. I finally convinced her to leave him and offered her the bedroom that you're using now. I helped her pack, and we were about to make our getaway when Ralph came home. Nat, I think we were both in danger. I've never seen anyone in such a rage. He turned all shades of colors and then suddenly passed out. I tried to save him, but he died quickly."

"Good," Nat said. "Sorry, but that's what I think. What happened next?"

"He never made a will and had no other relatives, so she inherited everything—the money, his possessions, the house—and there she stays."

"She's older than you, Aunt Carm."

"By more than twenty years. She's sixty-eight. She attended a junior college but has never held a job. She's floundering, looking for something to give her life purpose. Right now, she's decided to be a famous poet, although I don't think she's written anything. I've learned to love her, and I worry about her."

"No family?" At least Nat had her aunt.

Carm shook her head. "One other thing you should know. She may not be receptive at first to King Alfred, but she'll come around. She had a large dog when she was first married, but that brute of a husband killed him."

Noiselessly, Nat began to cry, suddenly feeling sorrier for Felicity than she did herself.

———◆———

Everything seemed foreign. The furniture, bric-a-brac, and ancient framed photos on the mantle were just as Felicity had left them, but nothing belonged to her. Well, she had been away for weeks, so it shouldn't be a surprise. But that wasn't all. It felt like someone had been there—someone who didn't belong. Not Carm, who had checked the house often, but someone else. Was there a different odor? Felicity shrugged. Her imagination had gone awry, as usual. She would unpack later. A cup of tea would be nice. Determined, she went into the kitchen, where she turned on the TV to block out the quiet rooms.

She was adding forbidden chocolate cookies to a platter when she was interrupted by a sudden news bulletin. *A woman has been arrested for child abduction at Aurora Memorial Hospital. Stay tuned for details.* Glued to the set, Felicity nibbled on a cookie, allowing the tea to grow cold.

When the report continued, the story seemed to have changed. Several policemen and nurses appeared with the reporter, and standing between two policemen, in tears and fiercely shaking her head, was Selena. Screaming nearby was Mrs. Usher with, presumably, her husband. The reporter addressed the camera. *There seems to have been a mistake made, and the hospital wants the public to understand that no child has been taken from Memorial Hospital.* The camera focused on the reporter's arms, where he was holding an object wrapped in a bundle. The reporter grinned and triumphantly held up a true-to-life baby doll. *Perhaps Miss Lopez is due an apology?*

"No!" yelled Mrs. Usher. "I saw her carrying the baby out. It was right before that bothersome patient in the next room left. I wouldn't be surprised if they were in on it together."

Felicity gasped. "Does she mean me?"

The reporter shook his head. "The baby Miss Lopez is accused of kidnapping is one of the dolls the hospital uses in its abduction drills. It is unlikely this particular abduction was even petty theft. The authorities will release Miss Lopez as soon as her citizenship is verified."

Poor Selena. Is that why she looked so scared? Nothing made sense, though. The Code Pink was yesterday, not today, and it was only a drill.

Her tea, now room temperature, was no longer appetizing, Felicity grabbed her hospital bag and trudged upstairs, suddenly finding the day too long and lonely. She thought briefly of a nap, but how many more hours could she stay in bed? She felt fine, really, just empty. Perhaps a hot shower would help.

Her bedroom—like the downstairs, no longer seeming to belong to her—had definitely changed. There were grocery bags on the floor and in the middle of the bed a blanket bundle. And next to the bundle was an envelope with the words, CODE PINK. Horrified, Felicity read the note inside—"Señora, you wanted to help."

Felicity grabbed her cell phone and texted.

EMERGENCY! CARM, COME AT ONCE!

URR

Code Pink

Selene to Ariadne

Delivery successful.

Chapter Three

"DAMN! NOW WHAT?" CARM PULLED over to read the text. "I'll have to go back. It's Flick. Some emergency. Do you want me to take you home first? We're almost there."

Nat shook her head. "No, that's okay. What do you think's wrong?"

"Could be anything—broken leg, hangnail—probably something to do with the plumbing. Will Al be okay a little longer?"

"Yes, he'll be lonely, but he's a good dog."

Carm turned around in a cul-de-sac and started on the return ten-minute journey to the west side of town. If this was what being a parent and caregiver was like, she was grateful she had avoided the whole marriage complication and that her ninety-year-old parents had died sensibly in their sleep. She supposed she didn't mean that last bit; it was hard at the time, although they were never a close family. Her parents were wrapped up in each other, and she and ten-years-older Charles were mere accidents. But really, how was she supposed to take care of an orphaned teen and a needy friend while holding down a demanding job and having any kind of life of her own? The three of them—four if you counted King Alfred—needed a plan.

"If she got hurt, Aunt Carm, wouldn't she call 911?"

"One would think. With Flick, who knows?" Life with Ralph had made Felicity wary of the police. Sometimes she had reported him and changed her mind when they came to the door. Right after, the cycle of violence would begin again.

Both retreated into silence. Not even two hours had passed since they'd left the townhouse, but it seemed much longer.

Carm opened the door. All was quiet on the first floor, but she could hear the television upstairs. "Stay here," she ordered Nat. "I'll shout down if I need you."

If there were an actual emergency, surely the television wouldn't be on. The bedroom door was open. "Flick?"

"In here, Carm." The voice sounded more excited than troubled.

"What the — ?" In the corner rocking chair, cradling an infant, sat Felicity, looking for all the world like a proud grandma.

"Flick, where did you get that baby?" Carm must have spoken loudly for the baby gave a jerk and a cry, and Nat came dashing up the stairs.

"Not so loud," Felicity warned. "He was on my bed." She soothed and rocked the baby back to sleep.

"Must I remind you that you sent for me?"

"I know. I'm sorry. Read the note." Felicity pointed toward the bed, and Nat retrieved it.

"Code Pink?"

"Read it." Felicity's eyes stayed on the baby.

"For heaven's sake, turn off the TV," Carm said.

"No, leave it. There may be another news bulletin. Please read the note, Natalie."

"'Señora,'" Nat read. "'You wanted to help. Please take package north toward Wisconsin. When you are far from here, call this number to learn what to do next.' Then there's a number and '*Te lo ruego.*'"

"I don't know what that means."

"I do," Nat said. "It means I beg of you. But I don't understand anything else."

"Someone came into your house and left a baby, Flick. We need to call the police immediately."

"No police. Selena trusts me to help. I will do exactly as she says."

"Selena was one of the aides in the hospital, right? How would she even know where you lived? Never mind. You told her, didn't you, Flick?"

"Maybe. I don't remember. We had a few conversations."

Carm scoffed. "You mean one-sided conversations, with you doing all the talking."

Natalie sat on the bed. "Selena. That must be the woman I met, Aunt Carm. She came into the waiting room and spoke Spanish to me. She was surprised when I answered back. Later, I looked out the window and saw her carrying a baby. It must have been this one. The blanket's the same color."

"The news report said it was a doll, not a baby boy," Felicity said.

"What?"

"That's why the TV is on. In case there's another news bulletin." Felicity told them of the earlier report.

"And you were mentioned?" Carm asked, concerned.

"Well, not by name, but it would be easy enough to figure out. That Mrs. Usher hates everyone, probably even her husband. You should have seen her face. Scary. She has it in for Selena."

"I'm thinking about Selena," Nat said. "She might be an illegal, and if this is her baby . . ." No more words were necessary.

"I'm calling the police right now," Carm said.

"No, wait," Nat said. "There's another bulletin. Turn up the volume, Aunt Carm."

"A baby doll was abducted earlier today from Memorial Hospital," the newscaster said in a jokey mode, and a clip was shown of what Felicity had seen earlier. When the newscaster continued after a commercial break, though, he was in a different mood. "What started as humor has taken a serious note. The nurses' aide, Miss

Selena Lopez, taken in for questioning about her immigration status, seems to have escaped custody. ICE agents are searching for her whereabouts. Anyone with information about Selena Lopez"—a photo was splashed on the screen—"should call . . ." A string of numbers was inserted under Selena's photo. "Police are also interested in interviewing the patients Lopez has served during the last few days."

"Still want to call the cops, Carm?"

"You can't, Aunt Carm, unless you want this little boy to be another lost baby, without parents or a home."

Carm shook her head. "I don't know what to do."

"I do," Felicity said. "Selena trusted me to take care of this child, and that's what's going to happen. You two must decide if you and your overgrown hound are going with me. But I'm going. It's time for me to start over."

"I'm in," Nat said. "I'm starting over, too." She and Felicity looked into each other's eyes, and in an inexplicable moment, a thrown-away teen and a wounded woman became fast friends.

> **URR**
> *Code Pink*
> *Selene to Ariadne*
> *In hiding.*

CHAPTER FOUR

"**O**KAY, BUT I DON'T THINK WE'RE doing the right thing."

"And what might the right thing be, Carm?"

"That's the problem, Flick. I don't know."

At that point, the baby started crying. Nat rummaged through the bags until she came up with a diaper, and in a cooler, a bottle filled with formula. "The right thing to do now is to make this little guy more comfortable. I'll take care of him while you two figure out how we're going to get out of here."

"You?" her aunt asked. "What do you know about babies?"

"Probably more than you. I've had tons of babysitting jobs." She took the squalling infant from Felicity and stretched him out on the bed. "I'm glad he's crying. He was so out of it, I think he must have been drugged to keep quiet." Nat proceeded to change a soaked-through diaper. "That's a nasty scar you have on your leg, little one. It looks recent. Well, Aunt Carm, we aren't sure of the right thing, but we do know it would be wrong to turn him over to people who'd make it impossible to find his family."

Finally, Carm nodded. It would be her job to figure out the logistics of driving to an unknown location with an abducted baby, a teenager, a recently ill, elderly patient, and a large dog.

Natalie held the baby and the bottle. Rocking gently, she began to sing.

Cierras ya tus ojitosuermete sin temor
Sueña con angelitos . . .

The song was long and beautiful. Neither Carm nor Felicity understood a word.

"Spanish, Nat? You speak Spanish?"

"Many people do where I live, Aunt Carm. I thought hearing it might be soothing. He might not be used to hearing English."

"It's lovely," Felicity said. "What does it mean?"

"Loosely translated: Close your eyes, little one, and sleep and dream while the angels watch over you. I will hold your hand, and when you wake with the morning, I'll still be here."

"I guess that's something we'd all like to hear," Felicity said quietly.

—◆—

"Your niece is not at all what I expected," Felicity chirped. "Funny looking with missing eyes because of all that wild hair, and wearing those oddly-matched clothes. But you can tell she's smart as a whip, knowing Spanish and how to take care of babies. Figuring out on her own how to get herself and a dog from New Mexico to Aurora. But the poor thing with no parents! She has her stepmother, of course, but it's not the same. I am sorry about Charles, and—"

"Please stop chattering, Flick. I know it's just nerves, but it's very annoying. We have got to plan fast before the police come knocking on your door. They're going to want to interview you, thanks to that wretched woman."

They had made their way to the seldom-used office that had been Ralph's sanctuary. In truth, Felicity had never entered it until he died. She kept all of her business matters there now, only because it seemed efficient. Carm shuddered. The room was as grim and immovable as the man himself had been—a cruel man and a cruel room. Someday soon, she would help Flick redecorate.

"We'll need money and a larger vehicle," Carm said. "I don't think we should go to the bank. I guess we'll use credit cards. No telling where we're going or how long we'll be away."

"Credit cards mean a paper trail," Felicity said, wisdom due to mystery novels and television shows. "I have plenty of cash here." She removed an unlocked strongbox from the bottom drawer. "I counted it once—over twenty thousand. I'm quite certain Ralph never expected me to have it."

"Flick, twenty thousand dollars in an unlocked box in an unlocked house?"

Felicity shrugged. "Who would guess? But won't your car do for the trip?"

"I don't think so. Two adults, one teen, a large dog—plus a baby who must be concealed and all the equipment that goes with a baby. And who knows if this house is being watched? We need to assume it is and proceed cautiously."

"One thing we should do," Felicity said, "is wrap an additional blanket around the baby and throw the bedspread into the washer."

"Overkill, Flick. We don't have time for it to dry. Your beautiful spread will be ruined."

"Doesn't matter. The spread wasn't my choice. Better that there's no sign of the baby if someone comes looking."

Their plan was risky, but they couldn't come up with anything better. Carm would drive into the open spot in the garage next to Felicity's car. Hopefully, no one would notice. It would be suspicious if Felicity were to drive anywhere so soon after being released from the hospital. Not a good idea anyway. Carm and Nat weren't under suspicion, as far as they knew.

"We'll pack the baby's equipment and whatever you're taking in the trunk," Carm said. "The baby will have to go on the floor in the backseat while you stretch out on the seat and cover yourself with a blanket. We'll drive into my garage to get Nat's and my things."

"Then what?"

"That's the part I'm still thinking about. We need to rent a van. And I don't think we can use cash to pay for it—too unusual. They'd want a credit or debit card to hold it."

"A check?"

"Iffy. Probably not."

Felicity went to pack a few belongings and the money. Fortunately, she hadn't had a chance to reinstate her mail and newspaper, so there was no one to notify.

Carm returned to Nat and was pleased to see the baby had fallen back to sleep. Drugged or not, it was easier on them to have him sleep.

Nat fell in with the plan immediately. "Good thing you've got plenty of time off because of me," she said. "Maybe I can be your cover story, in case we need one. You can tell people we're going to New Mexico to get my stuff—you know—south instead of north."

"And that's why we need to rent a large vehicle. Good idea, Nat."

"Except maybe you shouldn't say New Mexico," Nat said. "Too close to the border."

"No one would think we would be taking an undocumented baby close to the border. I think we're safe."

"I'm getting tired of calling him the baby," Nat said. "He needs a name, even if it's not his real one. I'm thinking José—Joey for short."

Joey it was, and soon the car was packed, with Felicity, uncomfortable but determined, covered on the backseat, on their way to Carm's townhouse.

"Thank God for attached garages and garage door openers." Felicity flung off the blanket and attempted to sit without stepping on the baby.

Nat hopped out, opened the back door, and rescued Joey, who peeked out from the blanket and gave her a wide smile. "Well, hello there, you cute thing," she said.

With an effort, groaning and stretching, Felicity left the car. "I am too old for this," she said. "Little Joey, you are far more patient than I."

"You'll need to be the babysitter while Nat and I pack," Carm said, as soon as they were inside.

Nat nodded. "He is in a happy mood and might want to play a little. I don't have much to pack, so I'll make up more bottles of formula. We won't be able to on the road."

"Right," Carm said. "Take an inventory of his supplies. We won't be able to shop locally, either."

All three recognized that whatever they had become involved in was certainly illegal.

"I need to let out King Alfred, first," Nat said. "Maybe I should walk him around the block, so that everything will look sort of normal." She opened the kitchen door, and out bounded the neglected dog. After a joyous reunion with Nat and Carm, he cautiously approached Felicity, who held Joey in her lap.

"Oh, do be careful," Felicity said fearfully. "Sit, King Alfred."

The dog sat, straight and still, awaiting further orders, with such a quizzical expression Nat began to laugh. And then Joey laughed, too. A charming, full-body, baby kind of laugh.

"Three guesses who the best babysitter is going to be," Carm said.

"Oh, the dear thing," Felicity said. "I meant Joey, of course, but it might apply to you, too, King Al."

"Come, Al, time for a walk," Nat said.

King Alfred gave a short bark. Walks were even better than babies in his estimation.

"So, Flick, what do you think of King Alfred the Great?"

"I may adjust," Felicity said.

Carm had packed her own belongings by the time Nat returned with King Alfred, who, after drinking a large quantity of water, plopped on the rug next to Felicity and went to sleep.

"I rearranged Joey's supplies," Carm said, indicating the piles next to the door leading to the garage."

"Once we add our stuff, we'll have way too much for your car, Aunt Carm."

"Agreed. Flick, I can't believe Selena hauled all of this to your house in one trip. She must have had help. Well, somehow we need to rent a van."

"A camper would be more like it," Nat said.

"A camper? My dear niece, you are a genius!"

"A genius?" Nat and Felicity said together, while Joey awake again, grinned at King Alfred.

Not answering, Carm grabbed her cell phone and punched a contact. "Hey, Bill! How's it going? That's good. We're fine, but it's complicated. It looks as if my niece will be coming here to live, but her stepmother is insisting we go to New Mexico and remove Nat's belongings. Yeah, she's a piece of work, all right. Well, there could be a lot to bring back, and I was wondering if I might rent your camper, if you won't be using it." After a pause, she smiled and gave Flick and Nat a thumbs-up. "Oh, my goodness, are you sure? Thank you! We're taking along my friend who just got out of the hospital, so it will be good she has a place to rest, at least for the trip down. Oh, that won't be a problem, that is, if I can store my car at your place. Terrific! Yes, I'll drive carefully. Thanks again, Bill. See you soon."

"Wow!" Felicity said. "I guess you struck gold."

"Your boss, Aunt Carm?"

"My angel boss. Not only may we borrow it—he refuses payment—he told me where he hides the key—no one home now. We can store my car in his garage."

"Where does he live, Carm?"

"About forty-five minutes west of here."

"So all we have to do is get there safely," Nat said.

"At least it's a positive first step. I hate that I lied to him, though." It was probably the start of many lies.

> *URR*
> *Code Pink*
> *Ariadne to Damon*
> *Package coming.*
> *Stay alert*

Chapter Five

"This is what we're borrowing? Your boss must really like you, Aunt Carm. Is he married?"

Carm laughed, hoping they wouldn't detect any bitterness. "Very much so, with three adult children and a few grandchildren."

"Whatever. It's absolutely gorgeous!"

Without incident, they had driven due west past Sugar Grove, not far from Aurora, but hundreds of miles away in terms of appearance and attitude. Sugar Grove was country, conservative, and the opposite of Aurora in every way. At Bill's farmhouse, Carm found the key right where he said it would be, and they immediately got to work transferring their belongings. Then Carm pulled her car into the garage.

"Bill calls it a compact mobile home," Carm said, "but it's big enough for us. And small enough for me to feel comfortable driving it."

"It's perfect." Nat examined every feature—a small kitchen and bathroom, plenty of storage space, and couches and chairs that converted to beds. Best of all, there was no separation between the driver and passenger seats, unless a curtain was drawn.

"Flick, you and Joey will need to stay in back with the window shades closed," Carm said. "Nat will be able to go back and help with Joey occasionally, but you shouldn't come up front."

Felicity agreed, and not just because the police might be looking for her. "I must confess I am weary. My doctor certainly would be displeased with me." Before leaving, she had used her cell phone to call him and a few neighbors to say she was going south with a friend to relax. "The sunshine and sea breezes will do me good," she'd babbled on the answering machines without giving any definite locations. Then she shut down her phone and removed the SIM card. "No one is going to track me," she'd said.

"Honestly, Flick. The things you know."

"Movies and lots of mystery books, Carm." And every quiz and puzzle she came across.

After a meal and diaper change, Joey obligingly fell asleep and Felicity settled back on the comfortable lounge chair. King Alfred couldn't decide whether he wanted to hunch down in the gap between Carm and Nat or lie down next to the baby. Finally, he stretched out near Joey and fell fast asleep. Felicity reached over and gave him a comforting pat. It was okay now. She would try to forget her own poor dog and offer this one her love. Perhaps, when all this was over, she would buy a new companion for herself. Felicity sighed. This was going to be quite the adventure.

"Aunt Carm, I've never had an adventure like this before."

"And I hope you never have again."

"I've never had any," Felicity said. "But what will we do if it ends right away? Maybe someone will come and get Joey after we make the phone call. I don't want it to be over too soon."

"I don't either, Aunt Flick. This is exciting!"

Carm burst out laughing. "Aunt Flick, is it? Both of you are a couple of kids. Well, I have the solution. If that happens, we'll turn the lie into truth and go to New Mexico for Nat's things. Now, I'd better watch the road. Soon, we'll head east and pick up the tollway going north."

Nat gazed back at Felicity. They nodded. Both wanted this grand adventure to continue as long as possible, and they were in no hurry to be parted from Joey.

⬥

Felicity dozed while their little house on wheels took them farther and farther from Aurora. Both King Alfred and Joey slept on, perhaps due to the steady motion. Felicity felt at peace. Perhaps being away was giving her this contentment, this feeling that it didn't really matter what came next. There were times she had felt that way in the hospital, but usually she had been too sick and uncomfortable. For the first time, she wondered if it might be wise to sell the house that still had Ralph's stamp throughout. Maybe buy a modern condo downtown—or even in a different town. There was Carm, of course—she wouldn't go far from her only friend. Could they consider living together? Felicity almost laughed out loud. She liked the notion but knew it would never work. Carm cherished her privacy. But Carm, Nat, and a large dog in one small townhouse? Carm might also be considering a move. Felicity closed her eyes again.

A familiar cellphone ring woke her with a start. Felicity grabbed for her purse. No, her phone was out of commission. It must be Carm's. They had the same ring tone.

"See who that is, Nat," Carm said from the driver's seat.

"Bill Egan, it says. Shall I answer?"

"Yeah. Put it on speaker."

Felicity shook her head, even though they weren't looking at her. "No," she stage-whispered. Nat looked back at Felicity pointing to the baby. Too risky. The loudness of the speaker could wake Joey, and if he cried, Bill would know there was a baby in his compact mobile home.

"Right," Nat said, understanding instantly. "I'll tell him you'll pull over. You need a break anyway."

⬥

"Yes, we're doing fine, Bill," Carm said heartily, although she was painfully tired. "Your house drives like a dream? Where are we? Not exactly sure, but we'll be heading west for a long time before we turn south. We'll need to find a trailer camp for the night. Is anything wrong?"

Carm listened, managing to stifle her growing alarm. "I see. No, I don't know anything about it. Yes, Flick was in the hospital at the time, but she had many aides; I don't think any of them stood out especially. Flick likes everyone."

Felicity and Nat stared at each other.

"Did you tell them anything about me? Oh, that's good. No, I don't like them either. We're doing fine, Bill. This trip is giving my niece and me a chance to know each other, and Flick will probably rest the whole way. Yes, it would be better for ICE not to know we're going to a border town. They might not believe it was a coincidence." Felicity and Nat gasped. Carm shook her head, frowning. "Thanks, Bill. Yes, I'll keep in touch. What? Just a second, Bill, Nat is trying to tell me something."

"Your phone," Nat whispered. "Bad idea."

"Oh, yes. Nat reminded me that my phone has been erratic. I'll be in touch but on a different phone. Yes, we'll drive carefully and stop often. Thanks again. Goodbye."

"ICE is looking for you?"

"Don't jump down my throat, Nat. Give me a chance to think."

Painfully patient, Felicity and Nat waited.

Finally, Carm grinned at them. "I'm hearing your forbearance loud and clear. Okay, this is what happened. It seems that ICE officers came to the pharmacy looking for me. I think it's okay. Bill pled ignorance. He just said I had taken a leave of absence because of a death in the family. Bill thought I had gone someplace south to be with relatives. Then they wanted to know if he knew anything about you, Flick. Bill said he knew you had been ill, but that he and his employees rarely discussed personal matters."

"That's all?" Nat said.

"Pretty much."

"Bill despises ICE agents," Felicity added. "They're in the pharmacy a lot, asking questions. Tell her, Carm."

"He has friends who have been deported. Most of us have had that experience or know of people who've disappeared. We are a sanctuary city, but most of the agents try to get around it. Bill gives advice about what doctors are safe or what over-the-counter meds might work for those who are too scared to see doctors."

"He's a good person," Felicity said. "You're lucky to work for him."

"Let me have your phone, Aunt Carm," Nat said, as Carm resumed driving. She pulled out the SIM card and powered off the phone. "We're down to only one," she said. "Mine. And we'd better keep it for emergencies."

"Funny how dependent we've become on cell phones," Carm said. "I feel kind of naked without one. Let's stick to back roads awhile longer. Probably safer than the tollway. Do you think it's okay to use the GPS?"

Felicity and Nat shrugged. They had no idea.

Carm drove on in silence. In the back, Joey stirred, and Nat crept back to change his diaper and give him a bottle. "I wish I knew how old he is," she said. "The way he reacts to things makes me wonder if he's older—just small for his age. I'll bet he should be eating baby food or even regular food by now. Something more than formula."

"Maybe when we stop, we should buy him something simple—like baby cereal, if we can find some." Felicity said. "I'm kind of hungry, too, aren't you?"

"Starving," Nat admitted.

Carm spoke at last. "We'll need to stop soon, anyway. You might be able to manage the bathroom while we're moving, but I can't. Besides, I'm not sure how it works. Do we have to be hooked up to something? Bill said that directions for everything are in the glove box."

Nat returned to the passenger seat. "I'll bet you're hungry, too, Aunt Carm. Do you want me to fix you something? Not that we have much."

"No, we'll stop. It's almost dark. This return to standard time is a nuisance. We need to figure out if we're going to stay at a motel or try to find a trailer park. The last won't be easy this time of year. To tell you the truth, I'm not even sure where we are right now."

Nat agreed. "I haven't seen any signs in ages. Let's stop at the next place that looks like it has food, even if it's just a gas station."

"Then I'll sit up front, and Nat can take my place," Felicity said. "It won't matter once it's dark. We must be close to Wisconsin by now. I'll make the call with Nat's phone."

"Oh, gosh, finally! Up ahead." Nat pointed. "A gas station. Food or not, they'll have bathrooms."

Carm pulled into a parking spot and stretched her arms. "We don't need gas, but if I don't stretch my legs, they'll soon be useless. And Flick, I don't think you should make that phone call until we know for certain where we are."

"We'll ask inside and buy a map, too," Flick said.

"You two go in first," Nat offered. "I'll watch Joey."

A loud yawn and a yip from King Alfred made them laugh. "I think Al wants to be first," Felicity said. "Go inside, Carm, while Nat gives Al a quick run. Then Nat can take my place."

With this shifting arrangement, they took turns and shortly were back in the camper, with Carm and Felicity armed with cups of coffee and a bag of donuts, and Nat with a chocolate bar, a coke, and a map.

"So we're in Hebron," Carm said, turning on the lights. Both she and Nat joined Felicity on the back couch. "Never heard of it. Have you, Flick?"

"No, but here it is on the map."

Nat looked over her shoulder. "Three miles from the border." She handed Felicity the phone.

"Oh, dear, where is that paper?"

"The front compartment of your purse. Right where you put it."'

"I'm too nervous. Your phone is different from mine. You do it, Nat."

The phone rang four times before it was answered. "URR," a male voice said softly. Nat returned the phone.

"Uh—hello, I was told to call this number." Felicity had never considered what she might say.

"Code?" the man asked patiently.

"Well, I don't know. I was told to travel north, and then to call this number about, uh, a package I have in my possession."

"Code?" the man repeated.

"A code? I don't know. Uh—maybe pink? Code Pink. Sorry, but that's the only one I know."

"Ah, yes. I assume you got away safely then. Well done."

"Thanks," Felicity said, pleased to be appreciated. "It has been a rather difficult day, and very, very long, especially since—"

"Flick," Carm whispered. "Don't chatter. Ask what we do next."

Felicity obeyed. "What are we supposed to do next?"

"You're not alone?"

"No, my friend is driving, and her niece is here, too."

"Three of you?"

"Well, yes, and the baby, of course, and a large Great Dane."

"Complicated," the man said, but he sounded amused. "Where are you now?"

"We're near Hebron," Felicity said, "at a gas station. I'm not sure what it's called."

"Kwik Stop," Nat whispered.

"Kw—"

"I heard. A little more remote than we expected. Look, hang tight. I'll call you back at this number in about a half hour."

Felicity started to argue, but the man hung up.

URR
Code Pink
Damon to Thalia
Approaching first station.
Contact with S lost

CHAPTER SIX

ORE THAN AN HOUR WENT by as they waited for the return call. All three had gone back inside the station for sandwiches, cookies, more coffee, and to use the bathroom. "Coffee goes right through me," Felicity complained.

"So stop drinking so much," Carm responded.

They were tired, irritable, and increasingly scared. And Joey, now that the motor home was no longer moving, was the most annoyed of all. He howled until his face turned red.

"I'll walk Joey," Nat said. "It's dark, and no one is around. I noticed baby food inside, but I'm afraid to buy it. If we're here much longer, the clerk is going to be suspicious."

"He probably is already. Go on, Nat, and take His Majesty with you."

"He's the best behaved of all," Felicity said. "I wonder if Joey would like to gnaw on a cookie. The ones I bought are plain enough. He could rub them against his gums. I think he might be teething."

"Oh, great." Carm shook her head at Felicity's offer of a cookie.

Checking her watch, Felicity sighed. "This might be the longest day of my life. I left the hospital nine whole hours ago."

"Oh, dear, how are you feeling, Flick?"

"Like you. Bone tired but surviving."

Ten minutes later, Nat reopened the side door, and the dog bounded back inside. Joey seemed to have calmed down, for the moment. "He likes walking," Nat said, "but the clerk was looking out the window at us, so I thought we should come back."

"I can't blame him for being suspicious," Felicity said. "Oh, come on, URR. We can't stay much longer. You said a half hour!"

"That's his name? URR?"

"I doubt it. Maybe it's a code. That's how he answered the phone—URR. Only URR I know about is the Underground Railroad."

"What? Oh, my God, Aunt Flick! Maybe that's what this is."

"Your phone is doing something funny, Nat. It's vibrating."

"It's the call, Flick. Answer it."

"Oh . . . Hello? I mean, Code Pink . . .Yes, we're still here, but the clerk in the station keeps looking out the window at us. I should have told you, we're in a camper—not a car. It's dark blue, but it will probably look black since it's dark now. Yes, I'll listen carefully. Okay, I understand. Yes, we'll wait. Goodbye. Thank you."

"We still have to wait?"

"He said it took awhile to figure out where to send us—because we're in a remote area. Someone will be here soon, driving a dark Fiat. We're to follow the driver. That's all I know."

"More waiting," Nat said glumly.

"I wonder how much longer it will be before the clerk calls the police. That's what I'd do," Carm said.

"I see headlights," Felicity said. "Here's hoping."

Nat made her way to the front while Carm returned to the driver's seat.

"Yes, it's a Fiat," Nat said, "and the driver is signaling us to follow."

"Like we have a choice," Carm said.

Felicity, who couldn't tell one car from another, except by color, was glad they knew. She held Joey close for her own comfort, and he settled down once he felt movement again. It could be a long night, she thought, wondering if he would stay awake after sleeping all day.

If this weren't the end of their underground railroad adventure, they needed to go shopping—for a car seat and baby food. Nat had discouraged her from giving him a cookie.

"Looks like we're going into a town," Carm said. "Maybe a hotel? I doubt if there are any trailer parks around here. Not exactly tourist mecca."

Another ten minutes passed before the Fiat parked at the curb outside a small, one-story house, and the driver got out and indicated that the camper should turn into a long driveway.

"A woman," Nat observed. "Not the man you talked to, Aunt Flick."

Foolishly, Felicity was pleased their escort was a woman. It seemed safer somehow. Three women against one, if it turned out they had made the biggest mistake of their lives.

The woman left the car and walked the rest of the way to join them. "You'll stay overnight here, but you must leave early in the morning, once you receive your next set of directions. Unpack only what you need, and then move your camper to the back. It's too big to fit in the garage. We didn't expect so many of you."

"We?" Felicity got a word in. "Who are you and they?"

"You don't need to know my name, and I don't know who *they* are." The woman looked at the sleeping bundle in Felicity's arms. "It's enough to know that we're trying to help this little fellow and others like him."

She led them into the house and turned on a few lights in the sparsely furnished living room. "You will find some food in the kitchen—perishables are in the refrigerator. Please use only what you need now, unless there's something that might be suitable for the baby on your journey. That you may take with you. Our funds are limited."

Felicity decided to leave a donation—maybe about what a motel room would cost. "Is there a phone here? How will we know what to do next? Will someone call?"

"No." The woman took a slip of paper from her purse. "Use your cell and call this number early in the morning. You will receive further instructions. I must leave now. Good luck to you." And before they could so much as thank her, she was gone.

"Me for the kitchen," Nat said. "Come on, Al. I've got your food. Let's see what's there for the rest of us."

<hr>

Felicity's prediction that the baby would not sleep proved accurate. The two bedrooms in the little house each contained two twin beds. Nat offered to share one with Joey and King Alfred. "I'll catch up on sleep in the camper tomorrow," she said. "I assume we'll be moving on. Aunt Carm, you've been driving for hours, and Aunt Flick, it would be horrible if you got sick again."

Gratefully and with few words, Carm and Felicity agreed. They made short work of bathroom routines and headed for bed. "I can't even think anymore," Carm said.

Nat found a jar of baby applesauce in the refrigerator, and Joey consumed the entire amount before polishing off another bottle of formula. Then she tackled a particularly nasty diaper. "Phew, you are a stinky, aren't you? I'm sure you must be older than you look. Now, how about a bath?"

Al whined, but Joey giggled. Nat thought it was Alfred's reaction rather than her words that caused it. Al was pretty smart and understood "bath." He hated that word as much as he loved "walk" and "out."

"We won't use the bathtub, Al," she said, after retrieving a towel from the bathroom. "We might disturb Aunt Carm and Flick. The kitchen sink will do just fine. Do you want to help me?"

Al stayed put until he realized Nat was going to the kitchen. Kitchens meant food, not baths, and he was too large for the kitchen sink. "Just right," Nat said, turning on the faucet and adjusting the temperature. "And the dish detergent is Ivory. That shouldn't do you any harm, little guy."

Joey loved his bath and gurgled with laughter as he splashed the water out of the sink. He was especially pleased each time Nat received a face full. Then she rinsed and dried his wriggly body and dressed him in a T-shirt and diaper. "You should be warm enough wrapped in a blanket, although you should be in a crib rather than a bed. I guess you'll have to sleep with me — if you sleep. And if we're going much farther tomorrow, we'll need more supplies." She'd start a shopping list: baby food, more diapers, baby shampoo and soap, powder, and a safer place to sleep. "Natalie won't let you go anywhere unless she knows you'll be okay," she promised, knowing that she probably had no power over the situation.

Nat walked and sang and rocked, until Joey finally succumbed in the twin bed next to the wall. Nat rushed back to the kitchen to drain the water and wipe the floor. What time was it? She checked her phone — 2 a.m. She'd charge her phone in the living room. Probably Flick would wake up first and need it. Then, finally, Nat, too, crawled into bed, keeping Joey sandwiched in between her and the wall.

Only a few days ago, heartbroken and angry, prepared to dislike everything, she had walked out of the Aurora train station. If it hadn't been for King Alfred, she would have run away. But she couldn't do that to him. Her old life was gone, and it no longer mattered. True, no one loved her, but the chances were good that her aunt might one day. Aunt Carm had been a surprise, and Flick an even greater one. Nat felt strangely drawn to the old lady, who talked way too much but was no stranger to the kind of sorrow Nat had experienced.

> *URR*
> *Thalia to Anteros*
> *Code Pink*
> *Trouble at source*
> *Breaking contact*

CHAPTER SEVEN

AT FIRST, FELICITY WONDERED WHERE she was. Shouldn't the nurse come in with her breakfast? But her bed felt wrong—mattress kind of lumpy, and the pillow awfully flat. She opened her eyes and saw Carm in the other bed, with the sun making an appearance through the east window. The adventure! She needed to make that phone call. Right now! But Nat had the phone.

She staggered into the living room, sleep deprived, but Natalie probably felt worse. Felicity had heard her with the baby long after she and Carm had gone to bed. It was too bad to wake her, but wait—there was the phone! Nat must have left it for her. Now, where was that paper? In her purse, of course. With confidence, she punched in the number, and a bored voice answered. "URR."

"Right. URR, this is Code Pink, awaiting further instructions." Felicity liked the sound of that. Like the lead in a spy movie.

"You must leave immediately. There's been some trouble. Your next stop is Madison. Then call this number."

"Just a second." Frantically, Felicity rummaged through her purse. "Okay, I'm ready." But she'd lost her part in the spy adventure, reduced to an incidental player.

"You're doing fine. Just relax." The voice, still bland but friendlier, ended the conversation.

———◆———

The camper continued to carry the rescuers and the rescued from station to station on this modern-day Underground Railroad. They took turns shopping at a Walmart near Madison. Carm made the major baby purchases—she was the only one likely to have an infant, although it was unlikely anyone in the store would care. Felicity was the banker. First, Nat went through the aisles and made a list, quoting the prices. Then Carm took the list and cash. With Nat able to follow the complicated assembly directions, soon the baby was in an expensive, regulation car seat that could be converted into a bed.

Purchased, also at Felicity's suggestion, were six pre-paid, disposable cell phones. "Carm needs to keep in touch with Bill," she said, "and we'll use the other burners for our URR calls." Nat's phone would be for emergencies only.

In Madison, another flat voice led them to an almost-empty RV camp, where they were finally able to figure out how the plumbing worked and how to convert the chairs into beds. Leaving Joey and Al with Felicity, Carm and Nat checked in at the main office. Both agreed to keep Joey's presence a secret, if possible, and they didn't know if dogs were allowed.

"Any more in your party?" the woman at the desk asked.

"Just my mother," Carm said. "She's not feeling well, so we're letting her rest." Carm then paid such a questionably small amount, she wondered if this were another URR safe house.

"Well, I hope she feels better soon," the woman said.

Later, back in the camper, Nat announced she was longing for a candy bar. "Anyone else? I saw machines in the office."

Both women shook their heads, clearly exhausted. Carm waved her out the door. "Don't be long, " she said. "We'll play with Joey until you get back." Nat gave a grimace and then smiled. It was going to be another long night for her, and she could use a sugar fix. But her aunts desperately needed sleep.

She was about to open the office door when she heard loud talking between the woman and a man, who'd not been there when they checked in. "So they didn't say anything about a baby? I don't think I like the sound of that. Are you certain they're the people we're expecting?"

"Well, they answer the description, and they seemed surprised by how little I charged. I couldn't very well ask if they were helping URR by transporting a baby, could I? I think they're being cautious—not a bad thing."

"I guess, but Emmy, the sooner we're done with all this, the better. I wish we never got involved in the first place."

Nat tiptoed away. No candy bar for her now. If it weren't so late, she'd think it would be smart to leave immediately. She wasn't certain why, but the man had given her bad vibes. Should she tell Aunt Carm and Aunt Flick? Maybe not. Both of them were weary, and everything seemed to be annoying Aunt Carm.

"No candy bar?" Felicity asked.

Nat shook her head. "Nice night, so I ate it outside. Just watch Joey for a few more minutes while I give Al one last run. Then I'll take over, I promise." Both women glared at her. Yes, it was going to be a long, long night.

◆

Joey slept the entire next day, as did Nat. Carm kept her eyes firmly on the road, becoming more and more certain they were doing the wrong thing and that it would not turn out well. "Underground Railroad," she scoffed. "How absurd is that?"

Felicity, alone and awake, remained optimistic. She was sorry that Natalie's days and nights were reversed. The two of them, both feeling useful, would have had much to talk about. Felicity sighed. Carm was being a good sport, of course, but Felicity wanted her to believe as well. This was their chance to make a difference—to do something positive.

After Madison, they were directed to Sheboygan, followed by Sturgeon Bay, the beginning or end of Door County, depending on your point of view. "Door County," Carm muttered. "How absurd is that? A peninsula bounded by a lake. Not exactly a destination for an Underground Railroad."

"Oh, hush, Carm." Felicity knew her friend was exhausted from driving, but she was getting tired of the negativity. Was she going to declare everything absurd? "I've always wanted to visit Door County—ever since I was a little girl." But we never went anywhere, she thought. Not when she was a child, and certainly not when she was married. Maybe that's what she'd do next. She had plenty of money, but would she be brave enough to go alone? Carm had been content with her boring, responsible job and only wanted to go home. Felicity eyed Nat, who was taking a break from her snooze and looking out the window. Nat might make a fine traveling companion.

"The leaves are gorgeous," Nat said, turning suddenly to Felicity. "It's not like this in New Mexico."

"I'm sure it's lovely there, too."

Nat nodded. "Yes, but it's different. I never really thought about it before, but I think I'd like to see the whole world someday."

"Maybe we'll do just that," Felicity said. But she patted Al, as if to assure him that anything they did would definitely include him.

———◆———

"We'll get to Sturgeon Bay early," Carm said. "It will be a relief not to drive so much today. I know I've been a bit of a pain, and I'm sorry."

"You've had to do most of the worrying," Felicity observed. "Nat has slept most of the time, and I've been treating the whole thing as a lark. I'm sorry, too."

"Maybe you can rest once we get there, Aunt Carm."

"It will depend on where they put us. I do need to call Bill. I won't mind watching Joey if you two want to explore. I hope it will be another campsite. That would be the safest, I think." Why she thought that, Carm wasn't sure. But there might be other people in Sturgeon Bay to help them—ones not connected to the mysterious URR group that gave them no real reason to trust.

The call to the next station was made once they reached the outskirts of Sturgeon Bay. Again, a voice saying URR, and Felicity proudly responding with CODE PINK.

"Yes. Well, there's been some trouble, so we're going to avoid the campsite we normally use. Proceed to outside of town, take Highway 15, then the roundabout to Route 6. There's an abandoned gas station at the intersection. A gray jeep will meet you there. It should take you about 45 minutes, but don't worry—the jeep will be there."

"Highway 15 to Route 6," Felicity said, gesturing to Nat to check the map. "We've got a GPS. Could we use it?"

"Absolutely not. Too risky. Proceed cautiously."

"Well, that was strange." Felicity reported the conversation.

"Something's off," Nat said.

"That's obvious." Without warning, Carm left the highway and turned down a country road.

"Carm?"

"Oh, we'll follow orders, Flick, but not yet. I'm going to call Bill first. We have no guarantee that the mysterious Mr. (or Ms) URR is going to tell us anything."

"While you make your phone call, I'm going to give Alfred a break."

"And I believe I'll stretch my legs. Fresh air would be good for Joey, too."

As soon as all four were gone, Carm studied the cheap, basic phone and punched in the numbers. Bill answered immediately. "Bill. It's me," she said.

"Bessie, how good to hear from you," Bill replied heartily. "I'm sorry I can't talk now. I have visitors. Are you at home?" Then, as if she'd answered, he continued. "Great. Look, I'll call you back about five. Yes, it will be wonderful to catch up. It's been too long!" Then, abruptly, the call ended.

Visitors who prevented Bill from talking? The police? ICE? It must be connected with her, or he wouldn't have bothered with subterfuge. What should she tell Flick?

The camper door opened suddenly, and they all piled back inside. Felicity, especially, seemed upset. "A man just called Nat's phone. He said the plans have changed. He seems to think our camper has been identified. But I don't think we've been followed, do you?"

Carm shook her head. "We've been the only ones on the road for some time, and we'd have heard a helicopter. Calm down, Flick. What exactly did he say?"

"Well, he gave me different directions—told me to return to Bill's, that someone there would take us to a safe house."

"All the way back? That's crazy!"

Nat had been thinking. "Wait, Aunt Flick. Start at the beginning. You never said Code Pink, like you usually do."

"I guess I didn't."

"Why?"

Felicity thought a minute and then gasped. "He never said URR!"

Then Carm told them of her odd conversation with Bill. "I assume he meant I should call him at five, since he wouldn't be able to tell the number of this phone. Nat, looks as if your phone is out of commission, too."

Al gave a short bark as if in agreement; Joey responded with a giggle.

"You're absolutely right, King Alfred," Felicity said. "Let me use a burner to call the last number I was given."

The normal routine continued. "URR," an uncertain voice said, and Felicity responded with CODE PINK. Quickly, she related what had occurred and then listened carefully. This time she had a paper and pen in hand and jotted down a number.

"I guess we're lucky anyone answered," she said. "No URR person called us. Our enemies, whoever they might be, know what we're driving but not where we are. And they obviously know Nat's cell phone number. Pull the SIM card now, Natalie. Otherwise, it will be only a matter of time before they track us."

"For Pete's sake, what did he say, Flick?"

"She. It was a woman. She told me not to use the phone number again but gave me a different one. She sounded more nervous than scared, but very worried.

"I knew leaving Aurora was a mistake. So what should we do now?"

"Proceed to the route, Carm," Felicity said, "but maybe we should stay off the highway as much as possible."

"Very well, but I will call Bill at five."

◆

Because of sticking mainly to back roads and getting lost a few times, it was close to dark when they reached the outskirts of Sturgeon Bay. Carm pulled into a combined gas station/convenience store. "It's just five," she said. "Before we go any farther, I will make that call."

"And I need to go inside before I break in two," Felicity said. "Joey is sound asleep."

Nat hadn't slept at all and knew she would be in for a long, hard night. "I should let Alfred run," she said.

"Wait, Flick. We're low on gas. Take some money and pay inside. It's pump five. Take plenty. I have no idea how much the tank will take."

It would be easier to talk to Bill without the rest listening, Carm reflected, hoping this time she'd be successful. Alone finally, praying that Joey wouldn't awaken as he often did when the camper stopped, Carm punched in the numbers.

"Bill, it's me. Is this an okay time?"

"Glad you figured out what I meant. Look, the ICE agents were back. They got my phone records and checked out all my recent calls. I think they know which one was your number—"

"My phone is out of operation now. I'm using a disposable."

"Right. But they checked the numbers from calls you had received back in Aurora, and I think they figured out your niece's."

"Nat did get a bogus call. We won't use that phone again."

"Good. I'm not sure what's going on, but you've got to be careful. I made the mistake of not telling Elle to be discreet, so she told the agents you were borrowing the camper and that you'd left your car in our garage."

Elle was Bill's wife. "Neither of you is to blame. Elle had no way of knowing—but what about my car? What did they do?"

"Impounded it. Don't know what they found."

Carm knew. Fingerprints, dog hair—that would be okay—but possibly blanket fibers, which might identify Joey, if they hadn't been careful enough. Flick's cautions had been wise. "We're taking good care of the camper, Bill."

"I know that," Bill said impatiently. "But that's not all, Carm. There's been a murder. The nurse's aid, who was taken into custody and escaped—the one who supposedly stole a doll."

Selena dead? "How did that happen?"

"She was found dead in an alley on the eastside. Knifed. No suspects."

Silence.

"Carmel, are you there?"

"Barely. I don't know what to say. Look, Bill, we have to make another call and hope we can get some answers. I'm not going to tell you where we are because I don't want to give you more problems."

"Don't worry about me. Even without you as a player, my activities are being questioned. You take care, and call again when you think it's safe or if I can help."

"Thanks, Bill. Be careful." But Bill had already hung up.

Carm sighed. Dear Bill . . . No time to think about him. Flick. She needed to tell Flick, and it would not be easy.

◆

Felicity began to cry, noiselessly, the tears streaming down her face. Nat's mouth quivered, and she held Joey tightly to her breast. "Joey's mother is dead?" she whispered.

"We don't know she was his mother," Carm said. "We're only guessing. Flick, I'm sorry."

Felicity wiped her eyes and seemed to pull herself together. When she spoke, it was in a voice Carm and Nat had never heard—determined and angry. "This changes everything," she said. "From the beginning, I've been behaving like a trusting child—assuming that the people directing us were acting honorably. Well, I say we start doing some directing of our own. Nat, you gas up. I put down a fortune; should be enough. You do that, and I'll make the call."

"Flick?"

"I'm all right, Carm. Just waking up after a long, lifetime nap. I'm going to call the mysterious URR on this new number. Chime in, please, if you think of something more to say or see me losing my nerve."

"URR."

"This is Code Pink."

"We've been waiting for your call. Have you arrived at the gas station?"

"Not yet. I have some questions first, and we're not going anywhere until they're answered."

"Go ahead," a man said.

Flick looked momentarily frightened, but Carm nodded encouragement. When Nat returned, both women cautioned her to be quiet.

"Well?" the man demanded, perhaps impatiently.

"Well, we've been going along without knowing anything about you. You're someone different each time. And the only person we've met was a woman back in Hebron, and she didn't tell us anything. I've figured out that URR might stand for Underground Railroad, but that's just a guess."

"Not a bad one."

"Okay. We seem to be in legal trouble back home. The woman who started us down this rabbit hole has been murdered. I've been scared—now I'm just plain angry. So before we follow more directions, I would like a guarantee that we will actually meet someone who will tell us what's going on."

"Can't say I blame you. Look, we're kind of shook up here by S—I mean, the murder. If it helps any, my name is Mike Young, and I knew the woman personally. Please follow the directions, Mrs. Sinclair. I promise that I will meet you and tell you as much as I'm able."

"Good. I will try to trust you for a little longer, mainly because I don't have much choice." Felicity hung up without saying goodbye. "Proceed to the route," she told Carm, as if she were a GPS.

"Wow!" Nat said. "Was that really you?"

Felicity shook. "I don't know yet," she said.

URR

CODE PINK

Adonis to Helois

Line Broken

Proceeding to Station #4

Await instructions

Alert The Griffon

"SELENA WASN'T JOEY'S MOTHER," MIKE explained the next morning, as they ate breakfast near the comforting fireplace in a cabin somewhere in the woods outside of Sturgeon Bay. "I met her a few times and was told she was one of our most valuable station masters." And a superb actress, Felicity thought. No way would she have guessed.

All were rested. As soon as they'd arrived, a woman, introduced as Helen, took charge of Joey, enabling them, especially Nat, to get a good night's sleep. "Talk tomorrow," she'd said, directing them to their sleeping quarters, one large bedroom. Numbly, they followed orders.

"Is Joey's mother okay?" Nat asked, mouth full of pancakes but eyes sparkling. Mike was, in her opinion, a hottie, and not too much older than she. Early twenties, maybe.

Mike nodded. "As far as we know, she's in Canada. We'll get Joey to her as soon as we're able. I have no information about the father. They fled Ecuador and have had a horrible experience, made worse by our own country."

"What's next for us?"

Thank goodness for Carm, Felicity thought. Always practical while she was too caught up in emotions right now to think clearly. Her brief period of rage was over, leaving sadness, but also a quiet determination. Selena—that sweet, shy woman, murdered, and, it seemed, an important leader in a dangerous operation. We all wear masks, she decided. None of us is what we appear. And often, our own country, as Mike put it, was the enemy. She shuddered before turning back to Mike, wondering what part of the conversation she'd missed.

"Your camper will be helpful," he said, "but we don't think you should drive it over."

Over? Over where? Felicity vowed to listen more carefully.

"It belongs to my boss," Carm said. "I can't let anything happen to it."

"Don't worry. One of our people is changing the license plates before a young couple will drive it over on the ferry. You'll go singly or in small groups in different vehicles."

Nat nodded, looking as if she'd go along with anything Mike suggested.

Carm shook her head. "I am not comfortable with that. In fact, I don't like your plan. We've turned over the baby. It's time for the rest of us to start home."

"No, Carm!"

"Sorry, Flick. Hate to ruin your grand adventure, but who knows how many laws we've broken? The person who abducted Joey was murdered, ICE is after us, and Bill might be in danger. I can't allow anything to happen to him—or Elle. Finish eating, and we'll get going. If we stick to main highways, we'll make it back late tonight. Unless you plan to detain us." Carm glared at Mike, challenging him.

Mike shrugged. "I'm not your jailor, even though I don't think you'll be safe. You're right—you've done your part. You brought us the baby."

Felicity gathered her courage. Yes, Carm had the stronger personality, but she was learning she could be strong, too. And Nat was looking at her pleadingly. "Mike, if there's a place for me to stay where you're going, I'd like to see this through. Selena entrusted Joey to me, and I need to find out what will happen to him." Mike nodded approvingly before she turned to her best friend. "Carm, maybe you should call Bill. If someone is trying to find the camper, you don't want to drive into trouble."

"Calling Bill is a good idea, Aunt Carm." Nat knew that if her aunt left, she'd have to go, too, as much as she wanted to stay with Flick—and Mike. She handed Carm one of the disposable phones—different from the one she used last time. Just in case.

It rang so long Carm almost hung up.

Then a guarded, "Hello?"

"Bill?"

"Look, I don't know how many times I've told you, I am not interested. I have all the vendors I need. If you don't stop calling, I will consider it harassment and contact Better Business. Never call here again!"

Carm said nothing. But she could hear a scuffling, and Bill whispering loudly enough for her to hear, "I've handled it." That was as good a cue as Carm was going to get.

"I am sorry you feel that way," she said, sounding as if she were selling snake oil. "All of my customers have assured me that our brands are far superior—"

"Who is this?" a gruff voice interrupted. Carm ended the call, as any brazen solicitor would do if confronted—she hoped.

"Carm?"

"Bill's in trouble, Flick. Nat and I simply must go back and see how we can help."

"And put your niece in danger, too?" Mike gave Carm a look that said clearly what he thought of her.

Carm began to cry silently. "I don't know what's right. Bill's in trouble, and it's our fault. I should never have gone along with this."

Then Carm's silent tears were accompanied by loud howls. Someone was crying his heart out.

"Joey," Nat breathed, just as Helen, the woman who had been caring for him, came into the room. He screamed and struggled while she held on tightly.

Then he saw Nat. He held out his arms to her. "Na-lee," he sobbed. "Na-lee."

"Does he want his nana?" the frustrated woman asked.

"No," Felicity said. "He wants Natalie."

"But we don't call her Natalie; we say Nat," Carm said, as frustrated as Helen.

"Natalie is what I say when it's just the two of us. Put him down, please. I want to see what he does. Come to Natalie, Joey." She held out her arms.

The woman obeyed. Stunned, Carm and Felicity watched as Joey, tentatively at first, but with growing confidence, crawled to Nat.

Nat held him, crooning in English and Spanish, "It's all right. Natalie will take care of you," until he settled down in her arms. "I won't leave him until he's with his mother again," she said quietly.

Felicity, Mike, and even Helen, nodded. Then a broken Carm nodded, too. "What should I do? I can't go because of Nat, but I can't stay because of Bill."

Mike seemed to come to a decision. "Helen, contact Athena. Tell her the Griffon needs to give us an update on Code Pink."

Helen gave him a dirty look before leaving the room.

Why the look? Felicity wondered if Mike had been indiscreet. Surely they weren't supposed to hear the code names. "Now what?" she asked.

"Now we wait. We must learn what's happening back where you come from."

Carm forced herself to calm down and approached Mike with something like sympathy. "You don't know, do you? You're kind of trapped, too. Everything is like a spy novel—on a need-to-know basis. Codes? Fake names? The Griffin? Athena? Perhaps I'm in a Greek myth. And that woman—is her name really Helen?"

Mike shook his head.

"Maybe she's Helen of Troy. What about you? Is your name Mike Young?"

"It is Mike, although my last name isn't Young. It seemed fitting because I'm the youngest one in our branch. At least I have been; maybe not anymore." He grinned at Nat, who blushed.

"Mike doesn't sound like a code name," Nat said.

"I thought you should hear something normal and real," he said. "I have a code name, but I'm afraid it's secret."

Felicity didn't point out that he'd just revealed some pretty important secret names. Odd how he pronounced Griffin—*on* rather than *in*, she thought as Mike left the room.

Nat stood. "I'm going to find out where they put Al, and then take him and Joey for a walk. You two want to come?"

Felicity nodded. "Stretching and fresh air might help. Carm?"

Carm shook her head. "I'll wait for Mike." She sipped her coffee and noticed it was cold, so she crossed to a side table where a hot thermos awaited her. She noticed Felicity watching. "Go for your walk. I'm okay, Flick. I promise not to do anything stupid." She smiled. "That's your department." Then she mouthed "Sorry," as Flick gave her a look.

◆

King Alfred was so delighted to be reunited with Nat that he stuck close to her as they walked side-by-side on a wide path through the woods. Normally, he would have bounded ahead, exploring and sniffing his surroundings.

"I can't tell where we are or in what direction we're headed," Nat complained.

"I think they did that deliberately. They made the route more complicated, even though it was dark, so we wouldn't know where we were."

"So that once we leave, we can't find our way back here again?"

Felicity nodded. "Although it wouldn't be a bad place to stay awhile. Plenty of room and good food."

"What do you think is going to happen, Aunt Flick? You know my aunt better than I do."

Felicity shrugged. "Not as well as I thought." She couldn't tell Nat—she could hardly admit it to herself—that it had always been about her, not Carm. How was Flick doing? How was Flick feeling? First, it was how could she get Flick to leave her husband? Then, how were Flick's finances, and should she stay in her house? Did she know Carm at all? "Carm cares a lot about her job," she said finally.

Nat grinned. "That's because of her boss. She's in love with him."

"Bill? Nonsense! He's too old."

"True. It is weird, but look at her face when she talks about him. Listen to her voice."

"But there's Elle. He's married."

"That is a problem," Nat admitted, "but it doesn't stop people. Don't worry. Aunt Carm isn't going to do anything about it. I think she respects their marriage. I'm just saying how I think she feels. She's worried about Bill; that's why she wants to go home."

"Maybe," Felicity said, although she wasn't ready to concede. She had never been in love, except with actors on television. "But Carm has always insisted on following the law. She's pretty rigid."

Suddenly, Al sniffed the air and bolted away. Nat laughed, causing Joey to laugh, too. "We must be near water. He adores water, as long as it's not for a bath." Joey squirmed, almost as if he wanted to race after the dog. "My arms are starting to ache," Nat said. "Aunt Flick, please carry him for a while."

"Of course." Felicity held out her arms.

"Ff-Ff."

"He said my name! You darling!"

"He's a smarty, all right. Come on, before Al is a soaked, muddy mess!"

King Alfred the Great was practicing his swimming strokes but greeted Felicity and Nat with triumphant barks. A bench on a grassy area was a welcome sight.

Felicity put Joey down. "Might as well see what he can do," she said.

"Ff-Ff," Joey said again.

"Don't forget Natalie," she insisted.

"Na-lee," Joey obliged, before crawling toward a bug.

"I wonder how old he is," Felicity said. "He's so tiny."

"Starting to talk and able to crawl—I think he's at least nine months; maybe more. He's just small for his age."

"I'm glad Selena wasn't his mother."

Both grew quiet, thinking of Selena, murdered in a back alley. What was happening back home?

"We should return to the cabin," Nat said finally.

"I hope we don't get lost. I can't tell which side of the peninsula we're on, can you?"

Nat shook her head. "I studied the map, but I'm totally confused. We're either looking at Sturgeon Bay or Lake Michigan."

"Well, you grab the king, and I'll carry Joey. Come on, little guy, let's go see Carm."

"Car?"

"That's right, sweetheart. Carm."

———◆———

"That's it, then," Carm said. "I don't have any choice."

"For now, anyway," Mike agreed. "We'll figure out something—in time."

Then Mike excused himself, "in order to get ready," he said.

Carm didn't ask, ready for what? She didn't care. She wanted to be alone for a long time before deciding what to tell Flick and Nat. The truth—eventually—she guessed. What else was there? Her coffee was cold, and she hadn't stepped outside this room all morning. At some point she should go to the bathroom.

"Aunt Carm?"

"Oh, you're back."

"Yes. Aunt Flick is freshening up. She'll be here soon. Both Joey and Al are napping. Al got soaked in the lake, and Joey's knees are all grass stained. He can say your name, too."

"Oh. That's nice."

"Aunt Carm, what's wrong? You've been crying."

"Mike showed me a video of children at the border, separated from their parents. It's horrible! Why do I persist in thinking our government is good and tells us the truth? You wait for Flick outside. I should go to the bathroom first. Then we'll talk. But not about what I saw."

—◆—

Outside the cabin was a picnic table. Felicity, who had wandered into the kitchen first, picked up a tray of sandwiches, cookies, and apples before joining Nat and, soon, Carm. Mike followed with a pitcher of lemonade and paper cups. All but Carm dove in.

"Carm, you should eat something." Felicity gave her friend a shoulder hug, which Carm ignored.

Half-heartedly, Carm picked up a half sandwich and took a nibble, not even noticing it was turkey, which she loathed.

"Aunt Carm, are you going to tell us what happened? Did whoever Mike talked to know anything?"

Carm took a sip of lemonade. "You start, Mike."

Mike cleared his throat. "Well, according to new sources, you can't go back—not yet, anyway. There's an APB out for the camper. According to authorities, Mr. Egan reported it stolen."

"Bill! That's ridiculous! He wouldn't do that. Carm got permission!"

"We know that, Flick," Carm said wearily. "They're on a fishing expedition."

"They?" Nat wondered. "Who are they? And what are they searching for?"

Mike shrugged. "Cops, FBI, Homeland Security, ICE—hard to tell. ICE has my vote, but they're all really on the same side. Just looking for anything they can find about Joey and Selena. More important, if the hospital is a player in helping illegal immigrants."

"It must be. One of the strange things Mike discovered, Flick, is that woman at the hospital—the one who was on TV—"

Felicity nodded. "Mrs. Usher, the one whose husband is on the hospital board. Both of them think they're God."

"Well, she's somehow connected with ICE, and she's sounding off a lot—in the newspapers and on TV. She's accusing the hospital of aiding illegal immigrants."

"Probably truc, but what does that have to do with Bill?"

Carm sighed loudly.

Felicity looked at her sharply, wondering if Nat's notion about Carm's feelings was true. "Is Bill in danger?" she asked Mike.

"We don't think so, as long as he has no more contact with Miss Abbott."

"Call me Carm. But you can't be certain he'll be safe. Sorry. I know you can't give that guarantee to anyone. My car was impounded, Flick. Plenty to find there."

"DNA, fibers from you, me, Nat, and—Joey. Even though we were careful, they'll probably find something."

Nat groaned. "Like the dirty diaper I put in the outside garbage can and an empty bottle in the sink."

Felicity patted her hand. "Not your fault, Nat. We were in a rush and not thinking clearly. Anything else, Mike?"

"Search warrants for both of your homes," Mike said. "They'll find the diaper and bottle, but they can't really connect you to Selena, other than you knew her at the hospital. But the connection with the baby is definite."

Nat shook her head. "There must be thousands of immigrants who have disappeared. I don't get it. What's so special about this particular one? Why put so much effort into finding Joey?"

"Good question," Mike said. "We're wondering the same thing. We've guided many people to safety and have faced danger each time. But I've never seen anything this intense."

"What's next for us?"

And the plan evolved. The camper would leave that evening. "A young couple who works with us will drive it and take the last ferry. The rest of you will be separated and go over a different way."

"Over?" Felicity asked.

"I'll show you on the map later," Carm said.

The maps. They were in the camper. What else was there that they needed? Felicity gave a start. Her money! While she doubted the "young couple" or anyone else would find it, she couldn't take a chance. "I'd like to travel in the camper with them," she said, looking at Carm in dismay.

Mike shook his head. "We've put on different license plates and innocent travel decals and a few political ones that no pro-immigrant would use." He grinned at that. "They're easily removed. No time or material for a new paint job but, Mrs. Sinclair, we can't have you connected with that vehicle at all."

"I think what's bothering Flick, Mike, is that we've got some things in the camper we're going to need. It's important that we get them out before it leaves." She held out her hand. "You have the key—not me."

"First, let me check if you can go inside." Mike stood. "I'm not the one in charge." He picked up the empty trays and went back inside.

"You're thinking about the money, Aunt Flick?"

Felicity nodded. "I think it best that no one knows about it but us. You can never tell."

"You can never tell," Carm agreed.

URR

Hermes to Adonis

Code Pink disbanded permanently

Proceed to final station

Extreme caution

MIKE RETURNED WITH THE KEY. "There's no one at the camper," he said. "I'll take you over. It's on the other side of the lodge."

Felicity hadn't known Carm had given up the key, although she'd assumed the camper was locked. If it weren't for the money, she wouldn't care. Guess this will be a good test of whether or not these people are honest, she thought. If they weren't, she, Carm, and Nat were in greater danger than ever.

Wordlessly, they followed Mike. Felicity guessed Mike wanted to make certain no one was there. He either didn't want them to see who was going to drive the camper or wanted to see what she and Carm were bringing out.

"I'll leave you to it," Mike said, but he looked at Carm worriedly.

Carm gave a humorless laugh. "Don't worry, Mike. I'm not going to make a getaway. Even if I wanted to, Nat would never leave King Alfred behind."

"I'm not exaggerating when I say leaving could mean your death—and not by us. Meet you back in the lodge." Mike left them alone, chilled and uncertain.

Carm entered the camper first. "You know, I might be tempted, if I thought we could get away with it. Especially since they've put on new license plates."

The plates were from Iowa, framed by a Dubuque car dealership. The decals, some old or aged, advertised fish suppers and BINGO. One said simply, FINISH THE DAMNED WALL!

"And where would we go if we did go back? Your house? Aunt Flick's? We wouldn't get away with it. Quick, Aunt Flick, check on the money. That's what matters."

Felicity, heart thumping, reached down behind the pots and pans in the kitchen cupboard, and finally lifted out a cloth bag. Just in case, she peered inside. "We're okay," she said. "I'm sure it wasn't discovered. Help me up, Nat."

Then Felicity gave each of them a stack of bills. "In case we're separated."

"Each of us should take a new phone, too," Nat said, distributing the three unused disposables. "We'll ditch the old ones."

Felicity put the remaining bundle of money at the bottom of a floral tote bag, covering it with medicine and makeup, and grabbed a small suitcase of clothing items. "That's enough for me," she said.

 Carm and Nat each packed a small bag, including maps of Wisconsin and a few personal items in order to cover their money. Al's and Joey's belongings were in the lodge already.

Carm locked the camper again. "Hope we see you soon," she said, giving the camper a pat. Felicity and Nat weren't sure whether she meant the camper or its owner.

Mike joined them for a simple supper. "If all goes well, the camper will leave for the island this evening. You will remain here for about a week." They didn't comment. What was there to say?

After dinner, without Mike, they walked King Alfred and Joey before putting both to bed. Then they settled down for a long evening in the lodge's main room that also served as the dining area.

Nat opened the map. "The camper is going here." She pointed to an island at the end of a long peninsula. "Washington Island."

Carm stared at it. "Tell me how that makes sense. If the goal is to reunite Joey with his mother in Canada, why would we go to a tiny island off Door County?"

Nat nodded. "I agree. I like and trust Mike, but the whole plan is crazy. Maybe he's being taken in, too."

That was possible, Felicity thought. They needed to be very careful. No one else should learn of the money. She wondered if the others had noticed that in order to get to the island, the ferry had to pass through a strait called "Death's Door." Just like back in the hospital, she'd be at Death's Door again.

◆

Carm lay awake. Sleep was seldom a problem for her, due, she thought, to a clear conscience. At least, almost clear. She'd tried to keep it a secret—even from herself—that she was longing for a married man, old enough to be her father. Well, she'd done the math, almost old enough. And she liked Bill's wife, Elle. They seemed to have a wonderful family that would suit her better than her own had. The main reason she wanted to return was Bill, and the main reason she didn't was Bill. "Please keep him safe," she whispered.

With all her heart, she wished she'd called the police when she first saw Joey. True, they probably would never have found out what happened to him, but she wouldn't have seen that horrifying, cruel video. She would have remained blissfully ignorant, as they obeyed the law and continued their shallow lives—with Flick in that overgrown, overly-masculine house, scribbling bad poetry, ignoring the obscenely large stash of money in her wretched husband's desk drawer. And she would remain in a small townhouse with an unhappy teenager and a huge, splendid dog, deserving of acres of land to run and roam. There was Carm's job of course—not always fulfilling but one that felt right to her. The thought of going back was frightening, but so was going forward. How could she trust these people with their made-up names and secret codes? Flick and Nat were wrong. This wasn't an exciting adventure. It was illegal and dangerous!

◆

Felicity couldn't fall asleep either, but that was no big deal. It was standard for her. Part of getting old, she had decided some time ago. It was always so hard to get comfortable. In bed, she became aware of muscles and bones that never troubled her during the day. It was harder to breathe, too, when the pillow wasn't quite right. If she didn't have to share a room, she'd turn on the light and compose a poem. She'd write about this intriguing experience. It had all the needed elements: mystery, danger, and fear. But also sorrow—and courage.

Sorrow, she thought, mentally putting aside the unlikely-to-be-written ballad. Poor Selena. Was she murdered because of Joey or something else? A back alley in Aurora. Felicity had never seen such a place. What was Selena doing there? It could have been a random, gang killing. Something to do with drugs. Selena was just in the wrong place at the wrong time. No, that theory was comforting but unlikely. Whatever had happened was about Joey and maybe other babies as well. Felicity thought of the aide's eyes, occasionally revealing that she was scrutinizing everything—that she understood English perfectly well, even though she pretended not to. Selena had risked her life for Joey and had trusted a stranger to take him to safety. Well, that was what she must do, even though she had been a coward all her life. "Enough is enough," people say when bad things keep happening, as if saying the words, instead of doing something, would make the troubles go away. But courage was what was needed. Probably sleep, too, if she were going to keep her wits about her and remain alert. In spite of her stern father and awful marriage, she had a tendency to trust everyone. That would never do!

◆

Finally, Nat thought, silently leaving her bed. They were finally asleep. She could tell by the serenade of snores—Aunt Carm's, occasional but startling, Aunt Flick's soft and breathy. She needed to check on Joey and King Alfred. Joey should be in the next room, if no one had spirited him away, and Al was shut in the pantry off the kitchen. He would not be pleased. She carried her jeans and shoes into the hall. After dressing quickly, she would explore the lodge.

It was, as she had guessed, empty. Mike, Helen, and anyone else who might have been there, were no longer. Should that be frightening? The cabin wasn't very large, of course—just the dining/kitchen area, the large bedroom, and a smaller one—no place for anyone else to sleep. The few closed doors she had thought might hide other rooms, concealed only supply closets. Alfred, with his sensitive ears, knew she was there, for he began his low whine that would soon turn into loud barks if she didn't respond fast. She opened the pantry door and received an exuberant paws-on-shoulders hug.

"It's okay, Al. Maybe we should go outside. You'd like that."

A quiet woof was the response.

"After that, you'll stay with me." Nat grabbed a flashlight from a hook next to the backdoor. "Let's find out if the camper is still there."

Nat was grateful to have the powerful Great Dane by her side. He was more comforting than the flashlight, for the moon was so bright she hardly needed it. The woods weren't spooky, but they were remote. If they were to leave, she wasn't certain which direction they'd take. Sure, there was the road that had brought them here, but there had been many turn-offs. She was convinced Mike and the others had confused them deliberately.

"The camper was right here." But it was gone now. Mike had said that would happen. They wouldn't know anything more until daylight. Surely Mike would return—if not for them, for—"Joey! Al, could they have taken Joey in the camper?"

Not thinking, assuming the worst, Nat rushed back inside, followed by an excited King Al, enjoying this new game. She flung open Joey's bedroom door. "Na-lee," he shrieked in delight. He was sitting up in his bed, wide awake.

In tears, Nat grabbed him into her arms. "Thank goodness you're still here!" She didn't think she had awakened him before but doubted she'd be able to get him back to sleep anytime soon.

"What are you doing?" Carm, followed by Felicity, came out of the bedroom.

Nat jumped. "I couldn't sleep," she said. "I guess you couldn't either. I started to wonder where everyone was, so I searched the house. And, well, it's just us. We're all alone."

"What?"

"It might be okay, Aunt Carm. We've got all the beds. There's nowhere else for anyone to sleep."

Felicity nodded. "I think this is probably another safe house. Mike and Helen must have gone to their own homes."

"Al and I checked outside. The camper is gone. Then I got kinda scared they'd taken Joey, so I came back, and—"

Joey grinned at them. "Na-lee," he said.

"I think we can forget about sleep," Carm said. "Any suggestions?"

"Food," Felicity said. "I'm hungry. Let's see what we can find." She held her arms out for Joey. "Come on, big boy. Anyone who can crawl and say our names should be able to eat more than formula and jars of baby food."

Nat grabbed a blanket from her bed and joined the others in the kitchen. She spread the blanket onto the floor. "Here, Joey. Practice your crawling. Keep an eye on him, King Al." Obediently, the dog wagged his tail.

Carm heated up two pots of water: one for instant hot chocolate, and the other for Kraft Macaroni & Cheese, their prize find in the pantry, suitable for all, human and canine.

After giving Al one more run, Nat announced that sleep might be possible. "But Al and I will stay with Joey." She and Joey settled into his bed, while Al stretched out on a blanket on the floor next to them. This time, all of them fell asleep, almost instantly.

URR
Griffon to all
stationmasters
Code Pink: destroy all links
Safe House 4 abandon
permanently

Chapter Ten

THE NEXT MORNING, NAT, JOEY, and Al were gone. Felicity didn't notice until breakfast. "French toast and bacon! Thank you, Helen."

Helen didn't answer, but when she turned around, both Felicity and Carm gasped. Helen's left eye was swollen, almost closed, and ranged in color from purple to black.

"Helen, what happened?"

"Nothing to worry about. Didn't watch where I was going."

"It looks painful," Felicity said. "Look, don't worry about us. We can serve ourselves and clean up. Put ice on that eye. You should have stayed home today."

Ignoring her, Helen headed toward the freezer.

"Nat and Joey must have slept in," Carm said. "I'll check on them."

"Yes, they should come before the food gets cold."

Felicity soon heard her calling. "Nat, where are you?" Carm stormed back. "They're gone! Okay, Helen, or whatever your name is, where are they?"

Felicity gasped. "Nat and Joey gone? How? Where?"

Helen shrugged. "I'm sure you'll find out in good time. They went with Mike early this morning, before I got here. Things are happening fast, and we're all getting out. I'll leave as soon as I clean up."

"But what about Flick and me?"

"Someone will be along soon. Best finish your meal, then pack."

"But—"

"Just do it, Carm. I don't think Helen knows much."

"But Mike said we would be staying for a week. Nat should have at least said goodbye."

Maybe she wasn't allowed to, Felicity almost said, but it was bad enough that she was thinking it.

<hr>

While that wasn't strictly what happened, Nat had been discouraged from awakening her aunt. "She'll try to talk you out of going with me, and there's no time," Mike told her. "Grab a quick bite, and we'll be on our way."

"How?" Mike didn't answer. Instead, he tapped a quick text and waited impatiently for a reply. Nat gave Joey the rest of the formula and wondered if they should buy more. Surely he was too old.

"Don't pack much. Take the diaper bag with you. The ladies will handle the rest."

"But—"

"No time. Our driver will be here soon."

"Who?"

"Not important. Pack!"

"Okay, but I'm not going anywhere without Al. He stays with me!"

"Right, the dog," Mike said. "I'd forgotten about him. Well, it's going to be a tight squeeze, but I don't suppose he could go with the others. You're going to have something to tell your grandpups, old fellow." He looked out the front window. "Our driver is here, so let's go."

"Where?" Nat demanded.

Mike looked around, out of habit, perhaps. "To the airport," he whispered.

<hr>

Carm picked at her food. "I don't like this. We're being asked to trust strangers with made-up names. You!" Carm glared at Helen. "What's your name—your real name?"

Helen filled the sink with hot water and detergent. "You don't need to know," she said softly.

Felicity removed her dishes. "Let's pack, Carm. We're bound to find out what's happening eventually."

"Mrs. Sinclair, you will take the baby's and dog's supplies." Helen pointed to a stack of bags in a corner. "A car will arrive soon to take one of you. Not sure which will come first."

Carm shook her head. "I don't like us being separated."

Helen shrugged. She had nothing further to say.

A car door slammed, and a man rushed inside. Good looking, Felicity thought, in a rugged, outdoorsy way. Young—about thirty. "Am running late," he said. "Name's Trey. Which one of you is coming with me?"

Helen looked out the window. "Small car." Then she pointed to Carm. "She is."

"Can't we go together?" Carm tried again.

Trey shook his head. "Orders are that you go separately. Safer that way." He looked at the luggage and bags. "Besides, car's too small for both of you and your stuff."

Carm was about to protest further, but Felicity stopped her. "It makes sense, Carm. ICE is looking for two women, a teen, and a baby. They might even know about the dog. Go along. Maybe you'll be with Nat first. Just take your purse and tote bag."

Carm, outnumbered, nodded, although it was obvious she was unhappy.

"Someone will be here for you soon," Trey assured Felicity. "Let's go, Carm. Temporarily, for a few hours at most, you've got yourself a new boyfriend."

⬥

"So it's just you and me, Helen."

The woman frowned.

"That eye looks painful. May I help—until my ride comes?"

Helen opened her mouth, as if to refuse, but seemed to change her mind. "You could re-check the rooms. We can't leave anything behind." She flinched suddenly, in pain, or possibly panic.

"Are you frightened of something?"

Helen nodded. "The sooner we're out of here, the better."

"Do you live nearby, Helen? We noticed you and Mike weren't here last night."

Helen nodded. "Live with my lazy, useless husband. Just help here when I can."

"That's good of you. And Mike."

She gave a slight smile. "We try. Let's check the rooms. Everything must be left spotless—just in case."

In case of what? Felicity followed Helen into the large bedroom, where, silently, Helen handed her a dust cloth.

Felicity examined the shiny dresser. "Looks fine to me, only we can't possibly eliminate all traces of our being here." Authorities could always find something that helped them capture criminals. In this case, she was one of them. What an odd thought.

Helen paused in her search under the bed, where she pulled out one of Felicity's handkerchiefs. "That's why another family is moving in as soon as we're gone."

"Another family."

"A couple with a teenage girl, a baby, a grandmother, and a large dog. Above suspicion with the right identity papers, including a rental agreement for this property. The younger ones will sleep in a camper similar to yours. Just tourists having a nice fall vacation."

"So someone did track us here?"

Helen shrugged. "I really don't know. You check the bathroom, and I'll see about the baby's room."

"That's why we're leaving early. Someone found out where we were." Helen clearly knew more than she was saying. "Helen?"

"Maybe. Mike mentioned last night that there's been another incident—possibly a murder."

"A woman?" Perhaps Helen meant Selena.

Helen shook her head. "No, a man. A doctor or something to do with medicine — maybe a pharmacist."

For one of the few times since her husband died, Felicity was speechless.

CHAPTER ELEVEN

"THIS IS HOW WE'RE GOING to Washington Island? Awesome! Wake up, Joey, and see the little airplane." Joey nodded drowsily and fell back to sleep in Nat's arms. "Oh, well, maybe you'll come to life once the pilot arrives." Nat looked around wondering, while Mike wrote another of his numerous texts.

Finally, he looked up and grinned. "The pilot has arrived." Nat looked around and saw no one. Then it hit her.

"You? You're the pilot?"

"My value to our rescue group. I'm the only one with a license. Now, all aboard."

Nat giggled. "I think that's what you say for trains."

Some coaxing was required before King Al consented to go into the back seat. "Let me hold Joey, Nat. Then you go first. Al will see that it's safe and climb in after you."

Al gave Nat a questioning look and a short bark before joining her in the backseat, where she gave him a treat. Then she crawled into the passenger seat and Mike handed over a still-groggy Joey.

"He's going to miss his first airplane ride," Nat said.

"Just as well, and I hope he and your dog manage to hold down their breakfasts."

Nat shrugged. Who knew what they would do? She wasn't even sure about herself. She had never been in a plane this small. But she held off comments and questions while Mike made the necessary arrangements before taking off.

"How long will it take to get there?"

"Not long—about a half-hour. Soon you'll be reunited with your home on wheels."

"And then Aunt Carm and Flick?"

"Yes, although it will take them longer."

"Then you'll go back to the cabin, Mike?"

"No, my job there is over. My home is on the island, so you'll see me from time to time."

Good. Nat wanted Mike to stick around. Her whole life had become uncertain. The only people she was sure of now were Flick, Carm, and Mike. Her head warned that she didn't know enough about Mike, but her heart said to trust. Sometime she would ask him how he had become involved. She thought his reason might be sad and personal.

———◆———

For a few miles, Carm and her driver, Trey, were silent. He seemed pleasant, but Carm remained alert. He acted too familiar—too jolly. Of course he might not know anything more than he had to drive her someplace. But why had their small group been separated? Surely it wasn't necessary. Perhaps she could ask a few basic questions.

"When will I see my friend again? She has been very ill and is my responsibility." On purpose she didn't mention Nat and Joey.

Trey shrugged as he attempted to pass an over-sized vehicle. "Damn trucks! They have no business on this narrow road."

Was that to be her answer? Carm waited.

Finally, as he saw the truck turn onto an even narrower road, Trey responded. "Sorry about that. Gotta drive safely if you're going to see your friend again. Am not pleased by the way this car is sounding—too many odd knocks. I'll stop at the next service station. No need for you to worry." At her look, which reflected more than worry, he added, "you're frightened. I get it. Just trying to do a good deed, and your whole life got turned upside down. You don't know if you should trust me—or anyone. Well, I don't know much, but I was told the plan was for you to be back with your friend by tonight."

"Where?"

"Where we're going now. Washington Island. You'll like it there. I'll say goodbye at the ferry, and you'll go over alone and be met on the other side."

"Couldn't we have traveled together in a larger car?"

Trey shook his head. "Best to split up. Not my decision, of course."

"Oh." Carm decided silence was a good option for now, especially since the car had pulled into a gas station, and that they were going south instead of north toward Washington Island.

◆

Felicity, of course, was her garrulous self and forgot to pay attention to the route leading from their hideaway in the woods. Oh, well, it was unlikely she'd ever return. Helen traveled with them. Their driver, who had failed to give his name, would take Helen home—or almost home. She insisted on being let off at a shopping center; she would walk the rest of the way.

"Thank you for your many kindnesses," Felicity said. "It couldn't have been easy for you."

"I do what is required," was Helen's short answer.

"She doesn't want us to know where she lives," Felicity confided to the driver from her position in the backseat. He didn't respond. "I suppose you'll take me the rest of the way to W—"

"Please," the driver interrupted. "I do not wish to know your destination. My job is to take you to your next contact."

"Well, all right. I suppose you know what you're doing, but I can't help wondering why everything has to be so mysterious."

Not answering, her driver turned off the main highway into a rest area, consisting of a picnic table, a few pine trees, and an outhouse. He began emptying the car.

"You get out here. Your driver will be along soon."

"Won't you wait with me?" Felicity didn't like him but disliked being left alone in this deserted place even more.

For a second, he seemed almost human. "Don't worry. Your driver will arrive the moment I leave. I'm not allowed to see who it is. I will send a text. Good luck to you."

Felicity didn't respond with words, just action. She walked to the picnic table, where she watched the driver speed away. What would she do if no one came?

But the driver kept his word. As soon as he was out of sight, another car appeared—an old green Ford, driven by a man closer to Felicity's age. Not handsome exactly—large, not fat, but muscular and weathered. Impressive, in control—this man had seen it all. "Mrs. Sinclair," he said, holding out his hand, "what a bewildering time you're having. I hope we'll clear things up for you soon." His eyes were a startling blue, piercing but kind. Like Paul Newman or "Morse," she almost said out loud. In fact, she controlled herself just in time. She changed her mind. Maybe he was handsome.

"My name is Felicity, but my friends call me Flick." Anything but Mrs. Sinclair, which always brought back memories of Ralph, but suddenly, her name seemed too—well—frivolous. She did not want this man to think she was a fluffy airhead.

"Flick." He smiled. "Unusual—short and to the point." Then he shook his head. "I prefer Felicity. It's more than pretty—it's joyous, hopeful. What we need these days. My name is Peter."

Felicity nodded. "Peter the Rock." It fit him.

He burst out laughing. "How Biblical! Well, let's get a move on." He held open the passenger door. "Make yourself comfortable while I pack your gear. There's a thermos of coffee for you, or water, if you prefer."

Peter started the ignition. "Now we can talk. There's a boat waiting for us."

"The ferry?"

"No, something more private."

Oh, dear, was she being too trusting again? Kind eyes and a soft voice could be deceiving. But there was no escape. "I need to rejoin my friends," she said. "It was my understanding we'd be together again soon."

"I'm sorry, Felicity. Didn't mean to make you more nervous. Yes, you'll meet at your camper on Washington Island. Natalie, her dog, and the baby, whom you're calling Joey, went with Mike in a small plane, Carmel will cross the normal way on the Ferry, and you and I will go over in a private boat. We thought you'd be safer if you traveled separately by different means and routes. You are right to be cautious."

And I'll stay cautious, Felicity warned herself. "When do you think we'll get there?"

Probably late afternoon, close to suppertime. Natalie will arrive first, possibly Carm second, depending on the ferry schedule. My family owns the inn next to where your camper is parked, so for tonight, at least, you and your friends will have dinner at our place. We only serve breakfast to our paying guests, so no one will be about."

"An inn? That sounds nice."

"It is. Right on Green Bay. We call it Water's Edge. Peaceful and lovely. Perhaps you will be able to relax."

Ruefully, Felicity laughed. "We'll see about that. Unlikely until I know Joey is safe and that we're not in danger."

Felicity had plenty of questions, but she thought they could wait for a few miles. Most of them concerned Bill. She couldn't dismiss what Helen had implied. Had Bill been murdered? What was happening back home? Peter seemed to know more than anyone so far, and she wondered if she'd at last met the one in charge. Could Peter be the Griffin? Might as well ask.

"Are you the Griffin?"

Peter choked on his coffee and when he recovered, roared with laughter. "What in the world makes you think that?"

"Well, you know more than anyone we've met, and you're not evasive. I think you could answer all my questions if you wanted to. And there's your appearance. You look like my idea of a Griffin."

"Please, I have a bit more hair, even if it is white. Yes, my nose is too long—almost a beak. In this case, though, the leader of our movement does not get his or her code name from your legendary bird. It's Le Griffon, with an *o* not *i*. The name comes from a sailing vessel, belonging to LaSalle, that sank in Lake Michigan in 1679. One of this country's deadliest shipwrecks. Never recovered. Just disappeared. Occasionally, adventurers think they've spotted it, but no one knows for sure. That's the way we want to keep our Griffon—undiscovered. If you think I resemble a 17th Century ship . . ."

"I guess not." But Felicity noticed he hadn't really answered her question. He hadn't said no.

CHAPTER TWELVE

CARM SAT INSIDE, ON GUARD, tote bag clutched to her chest, wondering what she might do if this were a trick and Trey not what he seemed—a young man with a name belonging in a soap opera or a Hallmark movie. Possibly they had driven south because he knew of this service station. The engine had sounded odd to her, too.

But after only fifteen minutes, Trey returned. "Looks like we're almost good to go," he said, smiling. "Some mysterious small part, and they took me right away. If you don't mind, I'll take it for a fast spin, just to make sure there are no more problems."

Carm stood, grabbing her bag. "I'll go with you."

"No need. Just stay put. I'll be right back."

Trying to keep suspicions at bay, Carm sat again. A waste of time, in her opinion, but she was not about to argue. Men and their cars were a stubborn force. Back to worrying, but at least, thanks to Flick, she had a phone and plenty of money. Pity she no longer had her smart phone, though. It was always good for entertaining and for keeping her from thinking, if not to relax. That she would not be able to do until they were all back in the camper. No, she would not breathe easily until they were in their own homes, and she had returned to her job with Bill. Why couldn't he talk to her? Most likely, something about Joey, but why so much concern about one small child? Couldn't ICE just say, "Win some, lose some," and move on to the next poor soul?

She was tired of the smells of motor oil and stale cigarettes. Waiting outside must be better than this. Surely Trey's test run must be over by now, but where was he? Probably talking with a mechanic about a mundane car part. She'd put a stop to that.

Outside, though, suddenly was filled with commotion. Police cars, fire engines, ambulances, all with piercing sound effects, raced down the highway. Clientele from the service station stood by the road watching. No wonder Trey was late, stuck in traffic, unable to return. Back to waiting inside, she purchased a local map from the woman behind the cash register, who paid little attention to anything but a talk show on her small television.

"Could you tell me where we are?" Carm asked. "I mean, what town?"

"Sturgeon Bay," the woman said, not looking up. "South side."

Not far from the route north after all. Trey had just wanted to check out his car at a service station he knew. She would wait patiently. No sense in borrowing more trouble.

——◆——

Joey was awakened by King Alfred's barks. "Na-lee?" he questioned sleepily and considered a spell of crying as he looked around at the unfamiliar surroundings. Then he spotted the camper. "Na-lee!" he yelled joyously, not seeming to mind its new decor. Al barked again in agreement.

Mike laughed. "I guess they both know where home is."

Going single file down a wooded pathway, Nat held Joey, Mike carried the few pieces of luggage, while Al pranced ahead to a clearing next to the bay, the new location of their home on wheels. Mike opened the door, and Al leaped inside to begin a serious sniffing inspection.

A squirming Joey demanded to be let down. He joined Al in a crawling search. "Car . . . Ff-Ff," he called.

"You're going to skin your knees," Nat said, scooping him up again. "We need to buy you some long pants. Carm and Flick are coming soon," she assured him.

"Hard to say which one will be first," Mike said. "It seems there's been a change of drivers. But you'll be back together by suppertime." He pointed in a northwesterly direction. At least, Nat thought he did. It was hard to tell directions here. "Peter, a friend of our group, co-owns Water's Edge, just on the other side of those trees. Tonight, we'll eat there and figure out what's next. I've got some stuff to do at the airport. Will you be all right if I leave you for a while?"

Nat nodded, although she wasn't in the least bit sure. Mike sounded too serious.

"I'll be back soon. It's okay if you want to explore a bit; just don't go far."

"Mike!" Joey blurted suddenly.

Mike's face lit up. "You're a smart one, all right." He shook his head. "Gotta wonder what's best for him. The longer we wait to take him to his mother, the more attached he'll become to us. But it's safer to let things settle down before we go to the next station." Shrugging, he gave her a sad smile. "Guess I'm glad I don't make the decisions."

Alone then with Joey, Nat felt lost. "How about we change your diaper, darling, and then stick you in some long jammies, so you can crawl around all you like? Natalie will see what there is to eat. Both of us are going to be hungry long before suppertime."

"Na-lee," Joey agreed.

———◆———

"There are goats on that roof," Felicity exclaimed. "How can that be?"

Peter laughed. "I'm surprised they're still there. You're lucky to see them. Soon, they'll head to their winter quarters."

"Goats," Felicity said, indicating more information was required.

"A major attraction of Sister Bay—the roof of Al Johnson's Swedish Restaurant. I wish I could take you inside for a bite to eat. Maybe someday."

"If I had my smart phone handy, I'd take a picture." Felicity was becoming fretful, not just because of too much stress in a short amount of time. Door County was beautiful, and they'd passed so many little towns that demanded to be explored. "I'll come back someday," she said, determined to stay pleasant. "If we aren't taking the ferry, where will we get a boat?" And what about all our stuff, she wanted to add, but thought she might sound as if she were complaining.

"Fowler's Bay," Peter said. "The boat is a small craft that will take us to a private harbor on Washington Island."

"But—"

"It's all right, Felicity. Here, look at the map. Someone will meet us at Fowler's Bay and take the car and your belongings across on the ferry. Someone else will meet our boat and take us to the inn. This is not our first operation. Please trust that we know what we're doing."

Guess I'll have to, Felicity thought. She'd settle back, enjoy the scenery outside, and inside refuse to worry. "Will we cross Death's Door?" she asked, pointing to a spot on the map.

"No, you'll be spared that." Peter reached into the glove compartment and pulled out two smaller maps. "One is Door County and the other is Washington Island. Might make things clearer."

But no one met them at Fowler Bay. Felicity observed a few homes in the clearings but mainly woods, without people or stores. "Kind of barren," she said.

"Privately owned," Peter said, without adding any further information. Felicity interpreted that to mean—none of your business.

At the small dock, a boat waited. Peter left the car with the keys intact and led Felicity to the boat—a speedboat, as it turned out. "Hold on to your hat," Peter said, handing her a raincoat.

Later, Felicity declared the ride the most exhilarating of her life, although she admitted to herself that didn't mean much. If she had worn a hat, it would be a feast for the gulls. Without the raincoat, she would have been drenched.

When they reached a small bay, presumably on Washington Island, she looked around puzzled. Sand and trees. Again, no people or activities. No one to take charge of the boat. Instead, Peter tied it to a post, but this time took the keys. "My boat. My keys," he said.

Felicity shook her head. "This couldn't be Detroit Harbor."

"No, that's too public. Someday I'll take you for a ferry ride. Now we'll walk to the road, where we'll be met, eventually."

"Eventually?"

"I can't use my phone here. No service. The island is like that."

At least, after a long trudge through the white sand that enveloped Felicity's feet, there was a bench. She felt every one of her sixty-eight years. She remembered what Ralph always said about his time in the Army. "Hurry up and wait. That's what we did every damn day!" Don't be like Ralph, she told herself, before sitting next to Peter and attempting to wait patiently.

—◆—

Still no Trey. Certainly the accident should have cleared by now. Although trying to keep a low profile, Carm decided it was time to talk to the mechanic, Guy, according to his ID badge. She would get nowhere with the indifferent woman at the cash register.

Outside, the apparent manager of the station talked earnestly to Guy. Thinking their conversation might pertain to Trey, Carm eavesdropped.

"Honest, Mr. Lester. I just replaced the accessory belt. The man complained of an odd knocking noise in the engine. I couldn't find anything else wrong. I was surprised that he wanted to give it a test run. I never found anything like a bomb!"

Carm ducked behind a truck. A bomb? Were they talking about Trey? Was that what the sirens were about?

Mr. Lester shrugged. "All we know, Guy, is that after you made a simple repair, the car exploded, and our client was killed. Prepare yourself. I am sure the cops will be here soon with questions you'll need to answer."

Guy began to stammer and shake. Carm, also shaking, managed to sneak to the back of the service station. Trey murdered? Might she have been the intended victim? She did not want to talk to the police, and she had no guarantee that Mr. Lester or Guy weren't involved. She had no help, except for a map and a cheap, basic phone that wasn't programmed with any numbers—no way to reach Nat or Flick. If only they had been thinking more clearly. But she had money—lots of money. Thank you, Flick!

Carm headed west, hopefully toward town and transportation to somewhere.

CHAPTER THIRTEEN

NAT WAS BORED AND ANXIOUS. An odd combination, she admitted. She and Joey had explored the camper and figured out sleeping arrangements. She unpacked what little she had and figured out exactly how the water and plumbing worked. She found a can of soup, which she shared, along with crackers, with Joey and Al. Then the three of them walked along the lake until they were exhausted. Joey and Al were now cuddled up together in one of the chair-beds, sound asleep. But Nat was fidgety and scared. Surely Aunt Carm or Aunt Flick should be here by now. Anything could have happened.

She studied the map until she was certain she could find her way around the island, which was actually one town, with shops, lodgings, and restaurants spread far apart. She hadn't even brought a book to read; a few were in the bags that either Flick or Carm had. She'd walk to the small bookstore in town, if she knew it was safe. But there was Joey. She could neither leave nor take him.

◆

Felicity sighed in relief when a car, driven by someone she hadn't seen before, stopped in front of the bench where she and Peter had been sitting forever. And it wasn't just any car, but the one filled with their luggage. Soon she'd be reunited with Nat, Joey, and Carm. Felicity planned to talk and talk until Carm came up with a rude way to shut her up. Peter had spent such a long period saying nothing that Felicity thought she'd go crazy. He wasn't exactly a small-talk kind of guy, given to revealing personal information. At least his silence caused Felicity to think carefully, too. Beware of being too trusting, she told herself, even though she liked this handsome Peter the Rock. Joey and Nat must come first; they were the innocents in this strange game they were playing. That means you're in charge—much too old to consider any romantic possibility. Peter is kind and extremely good-looking, but you thought Ralph was, too, when you first met him. Foolish to trust men, with your track record!

"Excellent, George," Peter said to the driver. "It was good of you to help us out. Any problems getting here?"

"All went smoothly."

Peter opened the back door for Felicity. "I hope you don't mind my rudeness," he said. "I must sit in front with George in order to direct him to our next stop. He won't be with us the entire way."

Felicity nodded, not concerned with politeness, but why wouldn't George, if that were his name, stay with them? Didn't URR trust anyone—not even friends? Trust. For days, that had been the most important word in her life. Trying to ignore Peter and George and the incessant beeping of texts coming from their phones, she gazed out the window at this strange land—totally flat and only six miles long. Carm and Nat could walk it easily. In width, a little over four miles—possibly she could do that if she ever got back in shape. She could see a few houses back in the woods, but mainly nothing, divided by forests and an occasional store or two. Finally, they pulled into the parking lot of an impressive building that declared itself a performing arts center. Really grand for a small island, she thought. The driver left the car—"I'll let you know if I hear anything, Peter."

Peter took the wheel. "You might as well stay put, Felicity," he said. "Not much farther now."

"Are we going to our camper or your inn?"

"Camper now. Water's Edge later," he said, before retreating into silence again.

But the silence was different now. Again, she had been thinking about herself and how she felt. Peter wasn't being indifferent to her — he was worried. "What's wrong, Peter?"

"Maybe you should come up front after all, Felicity. I have a few concerns, but I doubt they'll affect you. Let me give you a partial tour of my island. The grand tour must wait for another day."

◆

Carm felt as if she had walked for miles, although it was only two. Her feet hurt and her legs were scratched because of all the times she had retreated behind bushes or trees when she heard a car coming — and she was hungry. She couldn't possibly go to a restaurant, though, until she washed her face and brushed her hair. She tried to avoid crying but couldn't help it. Trey was killed, trying to help her. She hadn't liked him, but to be honest, she hadn't liked anyone lately, especially herself. She should have insisted on staying with Flick and Nat. Hell, she should have insisted on staying in Aurora! Everything was her fault, not theirs. Nat was a grieving child — and Flick was Flick.

Stop! You have money, even though your credit card is useless. You'll find food and a place to sleep tonight. You can pay for transportation, if you can figure out where to go. And you have a phone, once you to decide whom to call.

These thoughts were somewhat comforting. For the first time in her life, though, calling the police and requesting help was not an option. At the moment, she wanted to call Flick in, she supposed, Washington Island. She stopped. There was no guarantee that her niece and friend were there. Something could have happened to them, too.

Ahead was a small strip mall with a restaurant — burger, ham and eggs, Mom and Pop affair. Fortunately, some of her money was in small bills. Clean up in the restroom, eat, and then call the only numbers you know by heart — the pharmacy or Bill and Elle's home. Risky, but she had no other choices.

The restaurant was close to empty. The woman sitting at the cash register looked up in alarm. "Oh, my, are you okay?"

Carm attempted to smile. "I will be once I clean up, and then I really would like something to eat."

"Can you—"

"Oh, I can pay. Don't worry. I was in a slight accident. I look worse than I feel." Carm scurried into the restroom before the woman could question her further.

Thank goodness she'd packed a tote bag, in addition to her normal small purse. Hairbrush, make up, even a change of underwear, although she had thought that ridiculous at the time. She would need it wherever she awoke the next day. She scrubbed her hands and used paper towels to wash her face and wipe the dirt off her black jeans. After brushing her hair and applying makeup, she looked almost herself again. That wouldn't happen until she got rid of her panicked expression.

Back in the restaurant, the woman, Marge, according to the embroidery on her apron, looked relieved. "My goodness, you do clean up nice. What can I get you?"

A quick look at the menu. "A number 4, please." Probably more than she could handle. But she had no way of knowing when or where the next meal would be. "And I take my coffee black."

"Coming right up." Marge shouted the order from the kitchen door, and then returned to Carm. "Now, you said you were in an accident. A car? Need any help?"

Thinking fast, Carm shook her head. "No, I was hiking. I got lost, and I fell a few times. I'm okay, but I got hungry. I was awfully happy to find this place."

"Hiking." Marge eyed Carm's bag—not exactly something one would carry on a hike.

Carm laughed, hoping she didn't sound nervous. "I agree. This doesn't look like standard hiking gear. I'm meeting someone in town later and thought I might need to clean up. And I certainly did. Now, if I can figure out where I am."

"Depends on where you want to go."

Carm thought quickly, thankful she'd perused the brochures in the gas station. "We're meeting at the Third Street Theater."

Marge shook her head. "Closed for the season."

"I know, but my boyfriend works there. I think I must be just south of town."

"Right." Marge gave her a few simple directions that involved crossing a bridge and walking north. Fortunately, a buzzer from the kitchen interrupted further discussion. "Your food is up," she said. "Hold tight, dearie."

The number 4 consisted of ham, scrambled eggs, potato pancakes, and a small dish of fresh fruit. "Perfect," Carm said and asked for the bill. "I'll have to rush if I'm going to meet Larry on time."

Marge, possibly caught up in a vicarious romance, wrote up the charges. "I'll leave you to it, then. You have a wonderful evening, and no more accidents!"

Carm just wanted to eat slowly and then go curl up in her own bed. Instead, she ate quickly and thought carefully. As soon as she left the restaurant, it might be wise to change her appearance slightly. Just in case Marge was questioned by anyone. That was the scary part. Would the people responsible for Trey's death know she wasn't killed, too? Or wasn't she the intended victim? Maybe it was simply a horrible accident. She needed to call someone, but not here, with Marge definitely listening from the kitchen. Carm swallowed the last of her coffee, before leaving a generous tip along with the price of her meal on the table. Thank you, Marge, she thought. But, sorry, no goodbyes for us!

Evening was approaching by the time she reached the bridge crossing Sturgeon Bay. From her bag, she took a lightweight rust-colored jacket. Zipped up, it would cover her black and tan shirt.

Then she brushed back her hair and added a brown cap. Sunglasses, helpful with the sun lowering in the west, provided the rest of her barely adequate disguise. Once in town, she would find another stop and make a phone call to either the pharmacy or Bill's home.

Finally, on a bench at a bus stop, Carm pulled out the disposable burner. "Oh, Flick, no!" But seriously, it was her fault, too. This phone, never charged, didn't even include a charger. She wouldn't be calling anyone, until she bought a new burner. As she sat, considering her next move—possibly a hotel in town—a bus stopped and, to her amazement, Carm hopped on. Normally, she was not a spontaneous person. But this bus was going to Green Bay, which suddenly made sense. Staying in Sturgeon Bay, so close to where Trey had been killed was risky. A different large city, a decent hotel, and a fresh start in the morning—that was the best she could do today, other than pray that Nat and Flick were safe. Carm closed her eyes in this cold, dark bus.

CHAPTER FOURTEEN

SHAKING HIS HEAD, PETER JOINED the worried group in the living room at Water's Edge, his family's inn, run by his sister Astrid, her husband Lars, and occasionally himself. "Sorry," he said. "No one has heard from them."

Nat began to cry, as she had done periodically ever since Felicity had burst into the camper. "Where's Carm?" Felicity had demanded. Nat had shaken her head helplessly. After feeling abandoned and keeping Joey amused for hours, she was expected to provide answers? Now, at least, Joey was playing happily in a corner with the toys he'd found in a toy box. Felicity, pale but keeping tears in check, patted her hand, and King Al rested his head on her lap and stared at her with sympathetic eyes.

"Have you checked accidents from Sturgeon Bay to here?" Astrid wondered.

"Mike has made some calls. We'll have to wait longer for his report. No use speculating."

If it weren't for Carm being missing, Felicity thought she'd be almost content. The drive across the island was lovely, with many possible places to explore later. Peter had pointed them out. "If you walk down that path a bit, you'll come to an old Scandinavian church, an authentic Stavkirke. Back there is a tower you can climb. You'll love the stone figures tourists create on Schoolhouse Beach. And you must see the lavender gardens this summer." Fall was a grand season, too, according to Peter. He didn't have much to say about winter. Where would she be come winter? Peter seemed to assume she'd still be here.

The camper seemed like a secret hideaway in the woods, with Peter's family inn an easy walk away. Astrid, herself, was an advertisement for Water's Edge wholesomeness. Felicity was startled by how relieved she was when Peter introduced her as his sister, not his wife. Astrid might become a good friend, she thought, but first concerns must be about Carm. Surely, nothing had happened to her. Perhaps the ferry had been delayed. Peter seemed to be giving instructions. She needed to listen.

"Until we learn more," he said, "you two and Joey should plan on remaining at the camper. Al is a good watchdog. You can walk along the lake and in the general area, but stay away from the road and here."

Astrid looked about to object, but her husband, Lars, interceded. "Yah, too many guests coming in and out for you to be safe. I will deliver fine meals until we know."

"But what are we supposed to do?" Nat cried. Unlike them, she had been alone practically all day. "No TV, no smart phone, not even any books!"

Astrid pointed to a bookcase, mainly filled with worn paperbacks. "You're welcome to anything you wish to borrow. There are even a few baby books for Joey."

Felicity smiled. She badly needed a rest, and the books looked inviting; she was sure she could interest Nat in a few. Both of them should concentrate on something besides Carm. "I'm sure we'll be fine," she said. "Just find Carm."

And so they waited. Nat joined Joey at the toy box and kept her back to the group. Peter checked his phone and left the room occasionally. Lars said he had some work outside while Astrid thought she was needed in the kitchen. They were all on hold, Felicity decided, browsing the bookshelves, choosing a few likely titles for herself and Natalie.

Natalie. The child must be scared stiff—a young seventeen, with Carm her only living relative. Of course Felicity was worried about Carm. Terribly. But Carm was forty-five, and Flick was sixty-eight, supposedly a mature adult. All her life, she'd had to put herself first because no one else would—an indifferent mother, a cruel father, followed by an abusive husband. It was about basic survival. Then, finally, came a caring friend, who told her what to do. But Nat deserved better from the few adults in her life. No matter what happened, Felicity must keep Nat protected and safe.

Nat didn't look up when Mike, followed by Astrid and her husband, entered the room. Immediately, Felicity held a finger to her lips before catching Astrid's eye—a woman-to-woman silent plea, she hoped.

"Any news, Mike?" Peter said too loudly, Felicity thought. He hadn't caught the by-play. Or perhaps other things were more important to him than a teenager's feelings.

Nat spun around. "Mike! What happened? Did you find my aunt?"

Mike shook his head but kept his words light. "No news yet, but it's still early. She has a phone, right? I'm sure she'll call you as soon as she's able. Right now I'm starving. Any chance of a meal, Mrs. Nillssen?"

"Absolutely," Astrid said. "Natalie, come and help me, please. You can let your beast out for a run at the same time. Supper for Mike, and coffee and strudel for everyone else."

He grinned. "And for Mike," he added.

"Aunt Flick?"

"It's okay, dear. Just be helpful. I'll watch Joey." Joey wouldn't need much watching, for he had fallen asleep cuddling a stuffed panda.

Nat and Al left first. Astrid looked back at Felicity. "Thank you," Felicity mouthed.

Felicity took a deep breath. "Mike and Peter, before you say anything, I want to be sure you know something. Carm is Natalie's only living relative, but they met only recently, after Nat's father died. She is a child, and I want you to remember that. At the moment, you have other priorities, but you need to know that she is mine. Any bad news must go through me first. Do not talk in front of her."

Mike nodded soberly. "I understand. Well, the only thing I discovered is there was a bad highway accident on the east side of Sturgeon Bay. No details yet. No contacts on either side of the ferry from our drivers."

Peter stood. "I'll need the phone numbers for anyone Carm may reach out to. Risky, of course, especially since those people think you're headed to New Mexico. Let's hope she thinks to call Felicity."

At that moment, Nat rushed back into the room, eyes filled with fear. "Aunt Flick, I just thought of something! Aunt Carm can't call us! You have all the phone numbers. I don't think she even has a charger!"

Felicity's mouth dropped. Nat was right. Carm had a cheap phone without numbers and no way to charge it. She wasn't certain it had ever been charged. "At least she has plenty of money," she said, almost in a whisper.

Peter put his hands on Nat's shoulders. "From what I've heard, your aunt has a sharp mind. I will find her for you. I promise." He set down his coffee cup and gazed at the strudel with regret.

Felicity looked at one of the hardcover books she'd selected. Very old—perhaps an early English edition—a faded tan cover, printed with a red, star-shaped flower. "We seek him here, we seek him there," she whispered.

Startled, Peter turned to her. Then, grudgingly, he gave a half-smile before leaving.

———◆———

The next morning, Felicity tried to keep Nat from speculating. They played with Joey, explored with King Alfred, and talked and talked.

"Carm is a strong woman. I am positive she's figuring out a way to find us."

Nat shrugged. "Well, couldn't she just come to Washington Island? She knows we're here. Maybe take a bus or rent a car?"

"Rent a car with cash?"

"Okay, a bus or taxi."

"If a bus even comes here. Then what? Ask for you or me? Who would she ask? How would that work? She knows we were supposed to come here, but she doesn't know where exactly. She doesn't know Mike's real last name; we don't even know that."

"Peter?"

"She never met him. You did for the first time last night."

"Oh."

Oh is right, Felicity thought. She wondered if she should share the image she had of Peter as the Scarlet Pimpernel. A flight of fancy that probably wouldn't mean anything to Nat. Peter must be more important than he pretended. He was setting things in motion and would bring Carm back to them—if she were still alive.

"Aunt Flick?"

"Oh, sorry. I was just thinking that Peter and Mike and other people must be trying to find out where she is."

"What will happen to me if she's not okay? I don't have anyone else."

"You have me, and if you need to stay with me for always, that will be just fine." Later, Felicity determined, she must learn more about Natalie's past—what had happened to her father and exactly what her legal position was. But not now, for Mike was coming with their lunch.

"Have you found my aunt?" Nat demanded, before Mike had a chance to say hello.

Mike shook his head. "No, but Peter said he had a few leads. He took off late last night. I'm sure we'll hear something soon. No use worrying about it."

"We appreciate your bringing the food," Felicity said. "Especially for Joey." They smiled at the little boy who was pulling himself up Mike's jeans and insisting on being held.

They walked a short distance to a clearing in the woods, where there was a picnic table and a fine view of the lake. Large ham sandwiches for Felicity, Nat, and Mike, and various jars of baby food and apple juice for Joey. "I brought a package of teething biscuits for him, too," Mike said. "And a bone for His Majesty."

Al grabbed it and searched for a potential burying site. Nat ran back to the camper for cold sodas.

"I do have some news, Flick," Mike said, "but it's not good. We have a plan to distract Nat this afternoon. We'll talk as soon as she's gone."

"Flick," was it? Well, why not? Mrs. Sinclair seemed awfully formal, under the circumstances, and Flick is what Natalie called her.

As if she knew she was being discussed, Nat returned faster than they'd thought possible.

"Nat, Mike says he has a plan for you. He was just about to tell me."

"A plan?"

"And for Joey. Astrid will drive over soon. She and a few other women take care of a small group of children at our local daycare center. Children like Joey, whom we're trying to reunite with their parents. Only one of the women speaks Spanish, so you'd be very helpful. Also it would be good for Joey to be with other children."

Nat looked doubtful. "He'll need to take a nap."

"Yes, but so will the others. There are cribs there and diapers. Everything you need, really. Bring your dog, too."

"You want Al?" The dog barked in response.

"Especially Al." Mike gave him a pat, and then explained that a large gentle dog could provide important therapy to the children who had been traumatized by dogs. "Some of them had horrible experiences being attacked while trying to cross the border."

Nat nodded slowly. She had never thought about other children — other Joeys. "Al and I would like to help," she said.

◆

"Okay, Mike, what's going on?" Felicity and Mike returned to Water's Edge, now free of visitors. Mike poured them both cups of coffee.

"Prepare yourself for a shock." Mike paused, although Felicity thought she was almost shock-proof. "All we really know is that the car she was in exploded near a gas station on the outskirts of Sturgeon Bay. Her driver, Trey, was killed. We think it was a bomb. We don't know if the intended victim was Trey, Carm, or both."

"And Carm?" Felicity's hands began to shake, but her voice sounded normal.

"According to a woman who works there, Carm remained inside the gas station while the driver took the car out for a test. She wasn't in it."

Silence. What to say? Finally — "I guess that's something."

Mike nodded. "As far as we know, she's alive."

"But where is she now?"

"We don't know. Too bad she can't call you. Have you tried?"

"Over and over," Felicity said. "She doesn't pick up, and texts don't go through. But it's not just our numbers she's missing; she didn't take a phone charger, either." Felicity didn't mention that she didn't think the phone had ever been charged. It was the height of stupidity.

"So she might be conserving power. You say she has plenty of money?"

"Yes, several thousand dollars."

"That's good," Mike said. "At least she has access to food, lodgings, and transportation. She could even buy a new phone, depending — "

"Depending on if she's free," Felicity finished glumly. Thankfully, Carm had not been in the car when it exploded, but was she later captured? "ICE or the police may be holding her."

"They're pretty much the same thing these days. Peter doesn't think they've got her, though. Let's keep it positive for Nat's sake."

"Peter seems to be an important guy. Is he the Griffon, Mike?"

Mike grinned. "I have no idea. But do you think I'd tell you if I did? The Griffon's identity is one of the biggest secrets in URR." He shrugged. "Peter does seem to be high on the chain. I've known him all my life, and I trust him. That's what we should concentrate on now."

"I'll try." Felicity had trusted Peter, too, but she'd made mistakes before. She wondered how much she should even trust Mike. If the Griffon's identity was such a secret, should Mike have mentioned the code name? Of course, he was awfully young to be involved in whatever was going on. What to tell Nat must be her decision, not Mike's. "Any other reasons you thought Nat should go to the daycare center?"

Mike nodded. "I meant everything I said. She is needed. But she has become too fond of Joey, and he depends on her. I'm afraid it will be hard on both of them when Joey leaves to reconnect with his mother."

Felicity nodded. She had had similar misgivings—about her own feelings, too.

◆

Nat had nothing but fine things to report when she returned. "It's a great setup, and Joey and Al had a wonderful time." Their opinions would come later, for the two of them fell into instant naps, sharing the same small rug.

Felicity laughed. "I take it they didn't sleep much there."

"Could be a late night for me, but that's okay. We're going again tomorrow."

"You should take a short nap, too." Felicity wondered briefly what she was going to do with her time. Everyone was busy, except her.

Nat shook her head. "I probably should, but I think I'll take a walk instead. I was sitting on the floor most of the time, so I'm awfully stiff." She grabbed a small bag before heading out the door. "You would have told me if there was news, Aunt Flick?"

Felicity nodded. A part of her wanted to reveal everything, but most of her wanted advice—from Carm.

Nat pulled her hair into a high ponytail, although she didn't know why she was trying to disguise herself. No one knew her here. Perhaps she should have asked Flick to come along, she thought, as she walked down a twisty path before backtracking to the road. But there was Joey and Al to consider, and she didn't think Flick could keep up—or would approve of Nat's plan. It might be too late, but she needed to double-check what she thought she'd seen on the trip back from the daycare center. She had thrust three things into her small carryall: her wallet, her beater phone, and her smart phone. It had suddenly occurred to her that it was not useless, even without the SIM card. Making a call was too dangerous, as was using the Internet, even if she had Wi-Fi, but she could still take photos. And that was what she was hoping to do.

As Astrid had driven past one of Washington Island's small shopping areas, consisting of a post office, bookstore, and a coffee/gift shop, Nat had noticed a woman standing outside the post office. Of course, she could have been wrong—she'd had only a brief glance—but the woman seemed familiar. It was unlikely she was still there, but Nat would peek inside the bookstore and coffee house. Nat didn't think the woman had ever seen her, but she couldn't be sure. She might have risked telling Astrid, if she knew her better. If only Mike had been back at the camper, Nat would have confided in him.

She stood across the street from the post office. Not surprisingly, the woman was gone, for the post office was closed for the day. Outside the bookstore, a small group of people, having a lively conversation, had crowded in the doorway. Nat couldn't go inside without being noticed, but the coffee house should be safe enough. She took a few pictures of the surroundings, just to establish herself as a tourist, and added dark glasses to her disguise before crossing the street.

Another Cup was just crowded enough to let Nat blend in, she hoped, snapping a few photos of island-made crafts for sale. And then a loud voice seemed to drown out all others. "I really think we've spent enough time here, Arnold. Either no one knows, or they're all liars."

That was the woman Nat was certain she'd seen somewhere. Quickly, she took photos of both people, before wandering into a connecting room, featuring a seating area with newspapers and fliers about island activities. Another woman was in the room—one who caused Nat to turn away fast. She pulled some coins from her pocket and dropped them into a box for purchasing a Washington Island newspaper. It was Helen, whom she'd last seen in the cabin on Sturgeon Bay. A very different Helen, though, with a swollen face marred with cuts and bruises. When had that happened? Had Helen seen her, and did it matter? If she had, she was certainly pretending not to. Helen also turned her back and began frantically writing on a notepad.

"Reggie, get in here," shouted an unpleasant, gravelly male voice.

So that was her name, Nat thought.

"Coming." Helen pointed to the note still on a table, gave Nat a quick glance, and scurried over to the man, who had joined the couple Nat had photographed. She managed several photos of the foursome before grabbing the note and exiting out the back screen door. She would have enjoyed a mocha latte but no sense taking a chance of being seen. She began running and did not stop until she reached a wooded area.

Water's Edge was closer than the camper, so Nat stopped there first. Lars was talking to visitors next to the bay, but he excused himself when he saw her.

"Something wrong?" he asked.

Nat nodded. "Is Mike around?"

Lars shook his head. "Haven't seen him."

Nat sighed. She'd been running so hard her throat hurt. "Please try to reach him. Tell him to come to the camper. We've got an emergency." Without waiting for a response, Nat took off again. Suddenly, she was desperate to find out if Aunt Flick and Joey were safe. Helen's message had been short: *Tell Mike danger. They know.*

They know. The likely meaning of that, Nat decided, was that their enemies had tracked the group that had fled from Aurora to Washington Island. Nat shivered. The woods no longer seemed friendly. She was surrounded by something sinister.

———◆———

Felicity was anxious, of course, but also bored and slightly depressed. Since their journey had begun, she had grown used to being useful. Now, it was like the old days when she was irrelevant. Again, she no longer mattered. Carm was off on some adventure. Even if it was dangerous, she was involved. Unless—no, she would not allow that thought to continue. Carm would be all right; Peter would find her. And Nat had just gone for a walk and would return soon. Then the two of them would come up with some plan to help both of them during this interminable wait. Perhaps, she could help at the daycare center, too.

Joey muttered in his sleep, and King Al raised one eye to check on him. Satisfied that all was well, he quickly returned to his unsettling snores.

"Fine company you two are," Felicity said, returning to her book and her image of Peter as the foppish Percy Blakely, née the Scarlet

Pimpernel. Peter never said he wasn't Le Griffon; he just led his vessel down a different path, possibly to avoid collision—in other words, the truth. Mike hadn't answered her question either. Although in his case, it was possible he didn't know. What was Mike's story? How had he become involved in URR? How much did Astrid and Lars know? Everyone had a story, even her. Felicity sighed. She didn't want to be in danger, exactly, but she definitely wanted to be more than a bit player.

Abandoning her book, Felicity left the camper and wandered toward the inn. No sign of Natalie, but no sense in going farther— she couldn't leave Joey and his canine nanny. Head down, she returned and sat on a tree stump near the door, where she would hear Joey, if he awoke, and also be able to see down the path. Again, she tried to call Nat, but no response. They would have words about that, Felicity vowed.

"Aunt Flick" came the welcome cry, although it did seem overly frantic.

"It's about time," she scolded. "I was really getting worried about you—especially when you didn't answer your phone."

"I turned it off in the coffee shop," Nat said breathlessly, "and then I forgot to turn it back on. But you're okay, right? You and Joey and Al?"

"Just bored. Sit down and get your breath. Then tell me what's wrong."

"It's awful." Nat sat on the stump and took a few breaths while Felicity waited impatiently.

Finally, "Nat, I can't stand it anymore. Tell me before Joey wakes up."

Nat nodded. "Okay, I've got to show you some photos I took." At Felicity's surprised look, she continued. "On my smart phone. I kept it charged up when I remembered it can still do some things without the SIM card or Wi-Fi."

"I didn't know that," Felicity admitted. "Show me the photos."

First, Nat explained seeing a woman she thought was familiar. "I went back into town to check if she was still there. I'm not sure where I saw her before, but maybe you'll know." She showed Felicity the first photo.

"Aunt Flick?" Nat stood quickly as Felicity started to sway. She pushed Felicity's head between her legs the way she'd seen it done on television programs and waited for her to recover. "You recognize her, don't you?"

"Oh, yes." Her voice trembled. "That's Mrs. Usher, my obnoxious next-door neighbor in the hospital, and that's her husband, another loud-mouthed bully."

"But I don't think I saw them at the hospital. I just saw Selena and the nurse in your room when you left. How—"

"TV. That was the woman carrying on and accusing Selena of abducting a baby."

"Oh, right. And her husband was next to her."

"This is the last week of the tourist season. Perhaps they're just here on vacation."

"I wish. No, Aunt Flick." She scrolled further. "I've got a couple more."

"Helen," Felicity said dully. "Looking even worse than she did yesterday morning. Just bruises then; her husband seems to have added some cuts. She said she'd run into something. I didn't believe her—any more than Carm used to believe me."

"Mike and I left for the airport before she arrived. I never saw her."

"Has she betrayed us?"

Nat shook her head. "Maybe, but not intentionally. Her husband was there, too, with the Ushers." She scrolled to another photo. "Look, here he is. Doesn't he look brutal? Helen was terrified, but she did manage to slip me a note." She handed it to Felicity. I asked Lars to get in touch with Mike and send him here."

"They know," Felicity read. "But what and how much? I guess we should assume everything and wait for Mike or Peter. Then we'll need to establish some ground rules. We must be able to communicate with them if we're to continue with URR. At the moment, I feel like we're being used. I guess I trust them, but they're not giving us much reason to."

"Oh, I hear Joey," Nat said. "I'll take care of him, Aunt Flick. Here, I brought you a newspaper."

Felicity shrugged. A newspaper? Why would she care? But then a sudden thought, and she turned to the real estate section.

CHAPTER FIFTEEN

CARM HAD CRASHED FOR THE night at a Super 8 on Highway 43, the closest motel to the Greyhound bus station. It was adequate for her needs and next to a Kwik-Serve, where she could grab a sandwich, cupcake, and a cup of coffee — and, hallelujah, a disposable phone! Charging it probably would take all night, but at least she'd be back in business again. She thought briefly about using the phone in her room but couldn't risk Bill's phone being tapped, leading the enemy straight here. And it was late. Better to wait till morning. Carm stretched out on the bed with her supper and turned on the TV to a local station.

And at the top of the news was the story, although the reporter knew less than Carm did. Strange explosion. Authorities still not certain what caused it. Unidentified man killed. Woman, who had been with man earlier, missing and considered a person of interest. "I'm a person of interest, all right," Carm whispered. No photos of her or Trey, thank goodness. She had been worried about security cameras. The rest of the news concerned the nation, state, and Green Bay, in reverse order. The weather: wet and gloomy tomorrow. Most likely, she'd provide much of the gloom. Carm let the TV drift into a late-night talk show and allowed the voices to lull her to sleep. It didn't matter what they were saying; friendly human laughter was comforting.

◆

The phone rang and rang. Finally, a robotic voice declared the pharmacy closed but that she should leave a message. "In case of emergency," the voice said helpfully, "hang up and dial 9-1-1, or—" a phone number for another pharmacy in town.

Bill's pharmacy should not be closed. Not on a—what day was it? Not on a Friday! Carm's fingers shook as they tapped out Bill and Elle's home number.

The phone was answered instantly by—Elle.

"Elle, this is—"

"Bella! Of course I recognize your voice. Bill and I were just talking about you the other day. Bill isn't here now, but he'll be sorry he missed your call."

First, do no harm, Carm, she seemed to hear Flick's warning. Obviously, Elle knew exactly who she was but was pretending she was Isabella, Bill and Elle's daughter-in-law. The joke in the family was that they were Ella and Bella. And Isabella was married to—think, Carm—Andrew. Bill's sons were Andrew and Jeffrey. Jeffrey was a lawyer, living in a converted garage on Andrew's property.

"Andy and I were hoping we might see you this weekend."

"We were hoping that, too, dear, but I'm afraid that won't be possible until toward the middle of next month—the 15th might work. Maybe just me, though. I'll *shore* try to get it in *riding*, but you know what Bill is like—always at the pharmacy 24/7, although no use calling there this week. Inventory. I'll take the train to Milwaukee and one of you can pick me up. Fox Point is one of my favorite places. I *shore would* like to see you again. Oh, dear, someone's at the door. Give my love to Andy and the kids. Keep in touch."

"Will do. I'll call soon." But would she? Probably not. Whatever Elle had been rattling on about did not include contacting her again.

Carm wandered over to the Greyhound station and got a schedule before deciding if Super 8 would be her host for another night. There was a small lunch and snack area at the station, so she could sit, eat, and think.

She shivered. An early winter was predicted. Winter with all its holidays would arrive soon. But where would they be? Carm bit into the thick hamburger and looked with appreciation at the greasy fries. Grease was definitely what she needed, as well as the chocolate shake. Now for the phone call. It must have meant something. Was she back into the world of codes? "Yes," she whispered, taking a pen and pad of paper from her bag. What had Elle been trying to say?

Elle was warning her about the pharmacy. Don't call—too late! But the pharmacy never closed for inventory. Elle didn't want anyone to know that Carm was calling, so she pretended to be speaking to Bella, hoping Carm would remember her family members. Then came that weird message. Elle would try to go to Milwaukee on the 15th of December, and then to Fox Point. Carm grabbed her Wisconsin map. Yes, Fox Point was one of Milwaukee's northern suburbs; Maybe Andrew and Isabella lived there, but Carm seemed to recall Bill mentioning a different town.

Then there was that weird way Elle pronounced a few words. "I'll sure try to get it in writing." But that's not the way she said two of the words. She said "shore" and "riding," like she was a character in an old western movie. And she said shore instead of sure twice. "I shore would like to see you." Carm studied the map again.

"Shorewood," she breathed. That's where Bill had said his son lived, and it was the suburb just north of Milwaukee. Elle was trying to give her directions to Andrew's house. Back in the motel lobby, there was a computer for guests. Her next step was to find out the significance of *riding* and the numbers, *15, 24, and 7.*

Before leaving the station, though, Carm wrote a quick note and chanced taking a selfie on her disposable. She stood against a nondescript wall and pinned a sign on her chest. "I'm safe," the sign read. A click of the camera and the photo zoomed to Nat's old smart phone. Would it work? Would Nat even think to check a phone she wasn't using? Carm shrugged—worth a try. She'd send it to Flick's phone, too. Could a burner be traced? She didn't think so but wished she knew more about them. To be on the safe side, she returned to the Kwik-Serve and bought another.

No tickets were available for daytime trips, but at 9:30 that night, Carm finally boarded the bus to Milwaukee. From there, she would take a cab to 15 Riding Cross Road in Shorewood. Or perhaps she'd call first—414-247-1500—just in case this was another trap that might endanger Bill's family. After all, how did Elle know she was anywhere near Wisconsin, when she'd told Bill they were going to New Mexico?

Early evening, Mike and Peter returned together and tried to ignore that Felicity and Nat were frantic. "Whoa, Nat," Mike said. "Look at you, almost like a normal person—in fact a junior version of your Aunt Carm. It's great to finally see your eyes."

"Yeah, well, Aunt Flick cut my hair. It was starting to annoy me. But that's not important."

"We've been waiting for hours," Felicity said. "Did you learn anything about Carm?"

Peter collapsed onto a chair in the camper's kitchen. "Phew! Hold on! Give me a chance to catch my breath, will you. I'm a bit older than you two. How about a glass of water, and then we'll head to the inn for dinner. Mike and I have had quite a day."

Just having them back made Nat feel better, and she could tell Mike really liked her short cap of hair. Both men acted more tired than worried. "So what happened?"

Mike shrugged. "Peter and I had different tasks. I made a few deliveries—by plane. Exhausting but successful."

Nat nodded. Deliveries of undocumented immigrants to Canada, Mike meant. Someday soon, it would be Joey's turn. She would not think about that.

"Thanks," Peter said, sipping the water Felicity handed him. "That did the trick. Let's go before Astrid sends out the cavalry. Then I'll fill you in on what little I know."

"And I'll show you my photos," Nat said, holding up her phone. "I really hope you can rescue Helen and that she didn't tell the Ushers too much."

"What?" Mike grabbed it from her. "I think I'd better see right now!" He stared at Helen's face before turning the phone over to Peter. "Peter?"

"Yes," Peter answered the unsaid request. "Go now. Find out what she revealed." Without saying goodbye, Mike fled.

"Does he know where Helen lives?" Felicity asked. She recalled dropping the woman off somewhere near her house.

"I imagine so," Peter said. "He's known her for years. I'd better text Astrid not to hold dinner for us." He sent a quick text. "Now, let's look at your other photos." Peter scrolled through her phone. "So you went into the coffee shop, Nat. Probably not a good idea."

Nat explained seeing the familiar-looking woman outside the post office as Astrid drove her back from the nursery. "I decided to walk over to see if I could remember where I'd seen her before. I'd never met her, but Aunt Flick had."

Felicity nodded. "Her last name is Usher. She was in the hospital room next to mine, but I only spoke to her once; she was extremely unpleasant. Later on TV, she accused me of working with Selena. I have no idea why she thought that or connected me with Joey. This man," Felicity pointed, "is her husband. I think he's on the hospital board."

"And the other man is Helen's husband," Nat said. "Her real name is Reggie, and she's scared of him. He might be dangerous, but I couldn't tell anything else. He was just—there. That's it." She reached out to get her phone back.

Peter pulled the phone away. "Wait. Another picture just popped up." He stared at it, and then gave the phone to Felicity.

"It's Carm! Look, Nat, it's Carm!"

Nat gasped. The photo showed her aunt, standing against a brick wall and holding a sign saying, "I'm okay." Nat shook her head. "I can't tell where she is; she probably did that on purpose, just in case the wrong person got hold of this phone or hers. She took a chance that I'd even look at my old one."

"It wouldn't have occurred to me to check mine. I assumed that without the card, the phone was useless."

"Better take a look now, Felicity."

"Okay, Peter, if I can find it." Felicity went into the camper.

Nat felt shy talking to Peter. The two of them had never had a private conversation. She needed Mike. "Do you think Mike will return soon?" she asked.

Peter shrugged. "Hard to tell. It depends on what he finds. I am sure he'll report in regardless." He checked his phone. "Not yet."

"What's being done to find my aunt?" After all, Nat thought, that's what was important.

"I've set some things in motion back in Illinois. Please believe we're doing what we can." Then Peter gave Nat a piercing look. As soon as we hear from Mike, we'll need to change our strategy. Helen's actions mean we need to get Joey off this island and on his way to Canada."

"Not without me, you won't."

Peter nodded. "I figured you'd say that. Then that's what we'll need to do." He might have said more if Felicity hadn't interrupted, holding her phone.

"Sorry it took so long. I really had no idea where to find it, and I had to charge it a little. Look, I got the same picture. It gives the date and time. No phone number, though."

Nat wanted to talk about Joey, but she guessed she wouldn't. She thought that Peter had waited on purpose to be alone with her. He didn't want Aunt Flick to know about Joey leaving. The next move must be up to Peter—and possibly Mike.

◆

That evening, as soon as Joey fell asleep and Al was taking a badly needed long run, Felicity finally was able to talk privately with Nat.

They sat outside, where it was crisp and clear and the smell of pine intoxicating. How to begin, Felicity wondered. How could she make it clear to Nat who was in charge?

"Nat, it didn't escape me that Peter sent me to search for my phone so that he could talk to you alone. It's time for you to tell me what that was about."

"Uh—nothing, really. And he did need to see your phone because of the picture."

Felicity shook her head. "Sorry, I don't buy it. I might have, if both of you hadn't gone completely quiet when I returned. Nat, let's get something straight. You call me Aunt Flick, and until your real aunt returns and takes charge, I have that role. I am not a sweet little old lady you have to protect. Do you understand?"

"Sort of, I guess." Then Nat shrugged. "Maybe not. Peter is really in charge, isn't he?"

"He seems to be in charge of Code Pink, or whatever this operation is called, and I suppose he's in charge of Joey, although I'm not sure I'll allow it. But he is not in charge of you and me. Now what did Peter say?" Intentionally, Felicity sounded firm, realizing that Nat had heard her like this only a few times. There were good reasons Nat considered her a fluffy featherbrain.

"Okay, Aunt Flick. You've changed a lot since we came here. You don't talk as much, but when you do, it means more. It's hard to explain."

"You've changed, too, Nat. But let's leave that discussion for another time. No more deviating; what did Peter say?"

"Just that it was too dangerous for Joey to stay here, and that he'd have to leave soon. I sort of said that he couldn't go without me. Peter didn't disagree."

Felicity stood. She was growing angry but didn't want Nat to realize it. "I thought it might be something like that," she said. "Actually, Nat, you aren't going anywhere without me. And neither of us will leave this island until Carm returns. We might not have much say about Joey, but we'll try to keep him with us. We are the people he knows and loves. I don't think Peter's intention is to separate us further, but we won't take that risk." Felicity walked a few feet away, trying to decide how to say more. She stalled by saying, "Maybe you should call Al. We should go inside soon."

"He's okay. Not yet." Nat grabbed Felicity's hand. "Aunt Flick, are you saying you don't trust Peter—or even Mike?"

"Not exactly. I want to, but why should we? Trusting is not the same as liking. Carm didn't trust—or like—anyone we've met since leaving home; she went along with them because she didn't know what else to do. And now she's missing. I have to believe that she'll try to find us, but the only place she knows to look is Washington Island. We'll stay here, but maybe not in the camper. I found a few options in the newspaper you brought."

Nat gasped. "You mean, we'd just sneak away?"

"Hardly, although I wish we could. We can't even drive away safely. No, we'd need help. As soon as Peter and Mike return, I have some questions for them. How they reply will determine what we do next. Now, call King Al. It's time to go in."

———◆———

Carm arrived in Milwaukee later than she'd expected—after midnight. Too late to make a phone call, too late and dangerous to prowl around searching for a hotel. Instead, she threw herself at the mercy of her cab driver. "I'd really appreciate the help," she'd said. "A hotel close to the station, if possible." If things blew up, she'd get on a bus and leave—to anywhere.

"Well, the Hilton would be your best bet. They'll have rooms, although maybe not a single. Likely to be costly."

"That's okay," she said. "I can't be picky this time of night."

And soon, after giving the driver a hefty tip, considering the short journey, Carm found herself in an elegant room in a 5-star hotel. Thanks to Flick, money wasn't a problem, although the desk clerk was somewhat startled to receive cash rather than a credit card. He guaranteed a seven a.m. wake-up call. "No food available now, madam, but machines are located—"

She was as hungry as she'd ever been, but she was even more tired. A Hilton breakfast would be her next meal. After washing her face and brushing her teeth, wearing only her underwear, Carm collapsed onto the king-sized bed and was asleep in minutes.

Chapter Sixteen

Almost noon? Why hadn't the Hilton awakened her? The phone flashed its light on the bedside table. It seemed they had tried. Checkout was at noon. She had fifteen minutes to dress and leave, unless she paid more money. No, she didn't want to draw attention to herself. A shower was out. Carm threw on her clothes, washed her face, and then brushed her teeth again. She had hoped to use the telephone in the room to call Isabella. Well, that was out. Even worse, so was her Hilton breakfast.

But breakfast was what she wanted—not lunch. The pancake house down the street served breakfast all day. Might as well call from there, Carm decided, once the waiter had poured another cup of coffee and taken away a plate that had contained a large pecan pancake. Better find out if she had successfully broken Elle's strange code. If not, it would be time to consider a plan B. Rested and well fed, she felt up to the challenge.

Hand shaking, Carm tapped 1-414-247-1500. A man answered on the first ring. "Jeffrey Egan."

"Hello, this is—"

"Yes. We've been hoping you'd call. Where are you?"

Carm gave the name of the pancake house. "It's near the Hilton."

"I'll be there in twenty minutes."

"Wait—how will you recognize me?"

Jeff gave a short laugh. "I won't. But you'll know me. See you soon." He hung up.

That was odd, Carm thought, hoping the whole thing wasn't a trap. If life ever returned to normal, she was going to memorize many phone numbers. She knew the pharmacy, Bill's home, and Flick's land and cell, and Nat's. That was it. She finished her coffee and paid the bill. She would sit where she could see anyone walking in before they could see her.

◆

Lars visited the camper early the next afternoon to give Felicity some leftover sandwiches and the news that Mike and Peter had returned. Felicity thanked him but didn't encourage conversation. Hearing nothing for so long had worried her until her anxiety had festered into a deep rage. Natalie was busy taking care of Joey and other children at the daycare center. Felicity fortified herself with two large sandwiches and a cup of coffee. Then, time to take charge, she told herself, and marched over to Water's Edge.

She found Peter outside on the dock, gazing out at seabirds. "Peter, I see you've returned," she said. Then she gestured toward two Adirondack chairs facing the bay. "Suppose we get up to date? I have heard nothing for two days."

Peter smiled warmly but shook his head. "Let's just sit quietly and enjoy the beauty of the bay. I really can't say what's happening, Felicity, other than we're doing our best."

"Not good enough, and I don't believe you. Natalie and I are through with all this intrigue and will make our own plans. Perhaps we'll take a chance and go home."

"Oh, no, you don't. Too dangerous."

"Not your decision, Peter. I want to trust you. My instincts say I should, but they've failed me many times. I might be willing to risk myself but not Natalie—ever. Until Carm is found, she is my responsibility."

"Well, we do have a lead on Carm and a plan—or at least something in place. That's all I can say, unfortunately."

"Because you don't trust us," Felicity concluded. "I really don't know why. From the beginning, we've done what we were told. Selena felt differently, you know. She entrusted me with Joey's life when she knew hers was in danger. We left our homes, lied to our friends, and put our own lives at risk. Now one of us might be dead, but all you can say is that you have a lead. And you're still trying to separate us. I know you told Nat she could fly with Mike to wherever he's taking Joey."

"I told her—Well, I don't know about that . . ."

"Whatever, it's not going to happen. Nat and I will stay here together on this island until Carm is with us again. If she's alive, this is the only place she knows to look for us. I don't know what will happen after that. I have discovered places to rent, even furnished houses, and Nat, Joey, and I may go to one of them. Without your confidence, we will not remain on this property, and you might consider returning Bill Egan's camper. And I'd like a code name, too."

Felicity wasn't sure why she added that last bit. She was tired of feeling like an outsider. She tried to read Peter's expression. He seemed amused, without being condescending. He might even be proud of her. Unlikely, she thought.

"And do you have one in mind?"

"I do." Looking around first, as if there were enemies behind every bush, Felicity whispered in his ear.

Barely suppressing laughter, Peter cleared his throat. "An appropriate one, indeed, but as far as taking Joey, no. He's not your responsibility. You have no right."

"And you do? You have the authority to decide what happens to an undocumented child? I imagine the law wouldn't give either of us rights. Tell me, Peter, what you know about Joey. What does he like for breakfast? What is his favorite toy? What time does he nap? What song does Nat sing to him at bedtime? How many of his diapers have you changed? Does he call you by name? Do you really have more rights than we do?"

Peter smiled. "Okay, granted. But my group will be able to reunite him with his mother." Then he looked uncertain, causing Felicity to wonder. Did Peter believe what he was saying? Was he certain of the whereabouts of Joey's mother? She'd consider that later.

"Back to the point. You need to trust us, or let us go. Tell me what you've learned about Carm, or I shall go back to the camper, pack up, and call for a cab. I'll also call my lawyer."

"Very well, Felicity." Peter sighed. "I'll explain a little. We discovered that Bill Egan is part of a different group—one of doctors and pharmacists involved in their own underground railroad. Carm did contact him for help."

"Then both of them are alive." Unbidden, tears filled her eyes.

Peter patted her hand. "Yes, and safe, for now. We sent Miss Abbott a rather cryptic message on how to proceed. We just don't if she interpreted it correctly. And, unfortunately, we don't know where she is or what her resources are."

"She has plenty of cash, if that's what you mean by resources, and knows not to use credit cards."

"That is a relief."

"Peter, I assure you that we want Joey to be safe even more than you do. We love him."

"I know. If it were just me—"

"Your trusting me is enough." But Felicity knew she had many more questions. Her brain felt muddled. Later, she would write down those questions and find another moment with Peter. The first questions might be: Who is this child? Why are people willing to kill to find him?

For now, Felicity would relax. She'd give in to the moment. Yes, the light on the water was magical as evening approached. She and Nat might decide to have a simple supper, just the two of them, when

Nat and Joey returned. Then perhaps they'd come back later to see Lars lower the flag and play Taps on his old bugle.

Peter's phone rang. "Gotta take this," he apologized. "What? I'll be right there!" Ignoring Felicity, he ran toward his car.

◆

"Please pick up," Nat whispered. "Oh, please pick up, Astrid!" What would she do if no one responded? She could walk out of here and quickly find a place to hide, but not if she were carrying Joey."

"Water's Edge. How may I help you?" The voice sounded determined to be pleasant. Nat knew Astrid must have been rushing to finish her chores.

"Astrid, it's Natalie. We've got an emergency here. I just looked out the window and saw Mrs. Usher, the woman who is trying to find Joey."

"Tell Josephina. Take Joey and the children from away into the Rhine Room. Lock the door. I'll call Peter." Astrid hung up.

The Rhine Room — Nat had never heard of it, although she knew the immigrant children were often referred to as being "from away." Josephina responded immediately, and they hustled all seven children and Al into a back, well-equipped room. "No barking," Nat ordered King Al. Who me? his look said clearly.

Josephina locked the door. "Don't worry," she said. "The room is soundproofed." But Josephina seemed frightened.

Mrs. Fiske, a large Norwegian woman, adept at pretending she spoke little English, took charge of the regular daycare babies waiting for their parents to pick them up. Mrs. Usher would not get anything out of her.

"Does this happen often?" Nat asked Josephina in Spanish. She was hoping the woman would be comfortable, not as anxious, talking in her native language.

"This is first time," Josephina said. "It never happened before — I be here four years."

Never happened, Nat mused, watching Joey giggle as another little boy played fetch-the-ball with King Al. Why now? Why here? What was so special about Joey that caused Mrs. Usher from Aurora, Illinois to poke her nose into a small daycare center on Washington Island?

Josephina's thoughts must have been similar. *"Quien es este nino?"* she whispered. Who is this child?

CHAPTER SEVENTEEN

CARM SAT ACROSS FROM JEFF at the picnic table next to a roadside hotdog stand, still open late in the season. She shivered. It was becoming chilly. But it seemed safer eating here than going into a restaurant. Jeff had been correct. She identified him immediately. He was simply a younger version of his father. Oddly enough, he'd recognized her, too—"because of Dad's description." The way he said it let Carm know it was a compliment. She felt hopeful, but she needed explanations.

Jeff began. "I don't know a lot, but I'll fill you in on what I've been told. Dad had a nasty scare, but he's okay now—at home with Mom, who was far more frightened than he. He'll stay by her side for a while. A retired pharmacist in town is somewhat in charge of the store."

Carm nodded. "Rich Mayer—he's good. Bill was in jail?"

"Yes, but his sharp lawyer made short work of that. They really had no case—or proof that Dad had anything to do with illegal immigrants using the hospital. Of course, they might have discovered that he was helping them find medicine and doctors, but they didn't. Honestly, most police and lawyers in Aurora are on Dad's side. They've seen too many people they care about disappear."

"I should return to help at the pharmacy. They need me."

"Yes, they do, but no, you shouldn't. It's dangerous."

Jeff explained that a man named Peter had contacted his family about Carm being missing—"Peter was certain you'd would call Dad eventually, and the two of them developed some sort of code—one that would be safe—in case you did call. We didn't know if you'd be able to figure it out. Dad said you would, that you were plenty smart. I couldn't have been more relieved when you called."

"And what will happen now? Do my niece and friend know I'm safe?" Carm didn't say she'd sent a photo to their old phones. She decided to remain cautious.

Jeff shook his head. "I don't know. This man, Peter, seems to be in charge. At least he knows a lot, and Dad likes him. We are heading now to Washington Island. Once there, we're to pick up a message, addressed to me, on the bulletin board in the island's only bookstore, and give it to the store's owner. She's a close friend of Peter's sister and will help us connect. That's all I know. I feel as if I'm in the middle of a spy thriller."

"Tell me about it!" But they were on their way to Washington Island, which she knew was Flick and Nat's destination. Who this mysterious Peter was, she had no idea, but she would keep jumping through the hoops others had set in place until she was with them.

———◆———

It was night again. Felicity had been alone since Peter's abrupt departure. Nat, Joey, and Al had not returned, even though she had fixed a simple supper for all of them. Felicity took slow sips of her canned vegetable soup, not caring if it became cold before she finished. She shrugged when the bread seemed a bit stale. Being alone was frightening. Nat, Joey, Al, and most of all, Carm, had disappeared from her life. Forever? That's the way it felt. She started to cry.

"No!" she scolded herself before grabbing another tissue and blowing hard. "You're lonely, but at least you're safe—the others may not be." She was also good and angry, so some of the tears were from pure frustration. Whatever was going on, it was apparent she'd been forgotten again.

———◆———

Long after dark, the door to the Rhine Room finally opened. All of the children were asleep and most of the adults. Nat was still awake, even though she was so tired she hurt. Too many worries for sleep, she'd decided hours before. But the door was open. Nat leaped to her feet, uncertain whether she'd be facing a friend or foe.

"Nat, it's safe to leave now," a harsh voice whispered.

Thank goodness! "Peter!" Nat dashed from the room. "I don't think I would have lasted another second. Shall I get Joey? He's sound asleep."

Peter shook his head. "No, better that he stay here for a while. Safer, and there's no need to awaken anyone. Let's get you back to your Aunt Flick before she does something we all regret."

"She must be a mess by now. At least I had company. Aunt Flick didn't even have King Al."

"Oh, that's right. Your dog had better come with us."

Nat expected the camper to be dark and that Felicity would be trying to sleep, but the camper looked like a lit-up sausage, with its lone resident sitting on a lawn chair outside. King Al was the first out of Peter's car, dashing to Felicity and knocking her over in his joy.

Felicity was too happy to scold. Instead, she returned his slobbering kiss. "You're back," she cried, meaning both the dog and Nat.

Nat was shocked by Flick's appearance. She normally looked old, of course, but she didn't usually look sad and pale and worn. "My turn," she told King Al, and grabbed Flick into a hug. "It's going to be all right now," she said. "I promise."

Felicity shook her head. "Not until we find—"

Peter's phone startled them. "Yes, Astrid, that is good news. Yes, I'm sure we're hungry. We'll come right over."

Nat was startled by the smile Peter gave Flick. It was practically loving. When did that happen? "Peter?"

"Astrid said she picked up a package for us at the bookstore, and I don't think she meant a book."

A package? Nat managed not to gasp. She didn't want to fill Aunt Flick with false hopes, but she was becoming used to words not meaning what they should. When Mike talked about making a delivery, he meant flying people to safety. What if Peter meant something different by package? What if he meant—

❖

"Carm!" Felicity threw her arms around her missing friend and burst out crying. "Oh, I can't believe it!" She stepped back and looked Carm over from head to foot. "Well, you look okay. You're all right, aren't you? Truly all right?"

"I could use a shower. Then I'll try to look as good as you. Love the new hairdo, Nat."

"Aunt Flick is my hair stylist. She could open her own beauty parlor."

"Flick?" But that's all Carm said.

Felicity couldn't count the number of questions she had, but she knew Carm well enough to realize she'd have to wait for answers. Carm was like that. She needed time to process all that had happened. Then Felicity noticed a newcomer in the living room, a stranger. "Hello," she said. And then she stared. "My goodness, you look just like—"

"Bill," Carm ended the sentence. "Everyone, this is Jeff Egan, Bill's son. He's the reason I made it here today."

Jeff smiled. "More like your ability to crack an impossible code."

Felicity might have had some of her questions answered then and there if Peter and Mike hadn't entered from the kitchen.

"Mike!" Nat greeted. "You're back. Is Helen safe?"

"Yes, but in hiding now. She's had a dreadful time. But it's good to see Carm again. A regular reunion!"

"That you'll hold at the dinner table," Astrid yelled from the kitchen.

No further conversation. As Nat declared later, they were absolutely starving.

———◆———

While eating Swedish meatballs and Icelandic pancakes covered with lingonberries, Carm told her entire story from the bomb at the gas station to meeting Jeff in Milwaukee. "I'm amazed you figured out that code," Peter said.

Finishing a second cup of coffee, Carm made an observation. "I assume Joey's been reunited with his mother, and the rest of us can start home."

Felicity realized suddenly that Carm had no idea of their experiences while she was gone. She had little interest in Joey, other than seeing him as a problem that needed solving. Home for Carm was Aurora, her townhouse, and Bill's pharmacy. But that certainly was not the case for Nat or her.

Mike shook his head. "Not yet, but soon. We'll start off tomorrow morning. The plane is all set to go."

Astrid and Lars started to clear the table. "Not safe for the little fellow to stay longer," Lars said, before both of them left for the kitchen. They seemed to understand the group needed to talk alone.

Carm nodded. "Then it's going to work out fine for all of us. Jeff has agreed to drive the camper to New Mexico. Shortly before he arrives, he'll change the plates and try to get it looking as it did when it was in his dad's garage. Nat, Flick, Al, and I will take Jeff's car. We'll meet him at Nat's house and load up the camper with whatever Nat wishes to keep. Jeff will help prevent legal difficulties. Then we'll switch vehicles and return home. We'll start off tomorrow. Home, at last!"

Felicity and Nat stared at each other, and then, as if one voice, said, "No!"

"What?"

Felicity shook her head. "No, Carm. Nat and I must see this through. We are going with Mike to take Joey to his mother. We love him, and he loves us. We won't desert him now."

"But we need to go to New Mexico. That was our story when we left Aurora. Doing so might keep us safe. I really think—"

Mike interrupted. "I promised Nat and Flick they could come with me, and I could use their help with Joey. Once he leaves the country, I don't think you'll be in any trouble."

"And I doubt very much Felicity plans to return to Aurora," Peter added.

"No, I don't. I'll sell my house. My lawyer will take care of it. Nothing for me there but bad memories. I'll buy or rent something right here."

"I want to stay, too," Nat said quietly. "Al needs room to run, and I could keep volunteering at the daycare center. I wouldn't mind going to school here. Only fourteen kids in the whole high school this year—I'd know everyone!"

"But." Carm stopped, uncertain what to say.

"You could live with me," Felicity said. "Carm could come visit whenever she wanted."

Felicity tried to read Carm's face, never easy, but thought she almost succeeded this time. Carm looked frustrated, confused, but something more. Carm was relieved. Her townhouse—without a teenager and a large dog—her job, and her friend, Bill—truly the only life Carm wanted.

Jeff stood. "It sounds as if you're working things out. My time is limited, though, and I must start that long haul to New Mexico tomorrow. Mrs. Nillssen rented me a room for the night. I'll go cancel a few appointments and let you talk things over in private." Jeff smiled at Carm, and then started up the stairs.

"I should go, too, and prepare for tomorrow's flight," Mike said. "Nat, come with me. Let's take Al over to the daycare center. I'm sure Josephina would be willing to watch him until we return, and you can visit with Joey."

"What about me?"

"Just wait for me, Aunt Carm. When I return from seeing that Joey makes it to Canada, we'll drive to New Mexico together. Then I'll come back here to live."

"But—"

"You can have Peter's room, Miss Abbott." Astrid had returned for more dishes. "He has other places to bunk. Luckily, I changed sheets this morning. Come, I'll show you."

"That's fine," Peter said, "and Felicity, if you don't mind, I have a few things to tell you."

"But, Flick . . ."

"I'll come back to say goodnight, Carm."

CHAPTER EIGHTEEN

FELICITY STARTED TOWARD THE LOUNGE, but Peter held her back. "Let's take a drive. I'd like to show you something."

That suited Felicity fine. She was tired of being alone in the camper. But what did Peter have in mind? "Peter—"

"Did you mean what you said, Felicity? About wanting to stay here?"

"Yes, although I am wondering how you knew."

"Your choice of code names made me think you were ready for something else."

"Peter, I have more friends right now, right here on Washington Island, than I ever had in Aurora." Felicity gave a brief resume of what her life had been like.

Peter stopped the car. "You were abused?"

"Until my husband died, yes. You might say Carm rescued me."

"Then I guess I like her better." Felicity had guessed Carm hadn't made a good impression. "How does Nat fit into the picture?"

"She's still trying to figure that out." Felicity told him what she knew of Nat's past. "In a way, her father rejected her, and her stepmother doesn't want her. To be truthful, Carm doesn't either. Oh, she likes her and wants to stay in her life, but she doesn't want to live with a teenager and a huge dog. Carm was perfectly content until all this drama took over." Felicity did not tell Peter that if Carm had had her way, she would have called the police at the very beginning.

Peter shook his head. "Such sad stories. And you want Nat and Al to live with you?"

"Oh, yes. I'd love it." Felicity's eyes welled up. "To have a family would mean everything."

"It seems Nat feels the same way. Let's make it happen."

◆

What happened next was a gray Victorian house with white shutters and a wrap-around porch, located near Water's Edge and Main Road, within walking distance of the high school and daycare center. The yard was small, but the view of the lake and adjoining woods made up for it. Besides, Felicity thought, who wanted to mow lawns or shovel snow? And Al would be fine. He'd have the whole island for his run. Was it for sale?

"Let's go inside." Peter took a key from his pocket.

"Peter?"

"I thought you might be interested. I know the owner."

Felicity was certain the house spoke to her the moment they entered. "Welcome," it said. "I will be your home. You belong here." The rooms were spacious, and there was even a separate living area that included a small bathroom and kitchen, and a tiny room that could become a bedroom. Nat would have her own snug apartment.

"I stopped my friend just before he put it on the market. He has a position out of the country and must leave quickly. He'd even include the furniture."

"How much?" Felicity mentally crossed her fingers.

Peter named a figure that Felicity thought was far less than her Aurora house was worth. She nodded. "I'll need to sell my house first," she said. "Will he wait?"

Peter nodded. "That's what just about anyone would say. Give me the word, and you can move right in as soon as you return from your flight."

"Yes!" Felicity breathed. "It's my dream come true. And Peter, it's so big, we could use some of the rooms for the children from away—if needed, of course."

Peter gave her a hug. Felicity thought he'd been thinking that all along.

Instead of driving to the camper, Peter returned to Water's Edge, so Felicity could talk with Carm. "Before we go inside," he said, "I'll tell you what I found out about Mrs. Usher."

He finally trusts me, Felicity thought.

❖

Nat and Felicity sat in Peter's room, now occupied by Carm. It was more of a suite, Nat thought, wondering about the other places Peter might stay. He was definitely a man of mystery.

"You understand why we must go with Joey, don't you, Carm?"

Carm shook her head. "I don't know, Flick. Not really, but obviously both of you are determined."

"In a way, I promised Selena."

"Both of us love Joey," Nat said. "We need to know that he reaches his mother safely. And it would be hard for Mike to travel alone with him." She didn't add that he probably did things like that all the time, but why give Aunt Carm more reasons to object?

"Okay, I'll wait for you to return, and then we'll drive to New Mexico. I wish you'd come, too, Flick."

"Sorry, I've found my place." Felicity told them about the house she intended to purchase. "You can visit me and Nat."

"It sounds perfect," Nat breathed.

Carm yawned. "Well, if you're happy, I guess I am, too. If it doesn't work out, you can always come home. That's where I'll be. Home to stay! Now, if you don't mind, I'm going to finally take that long, hot shower, and then go to bed. I'll see the two of you when you return."

"One more thing, Aunt Carm. I was just wondering . . ." Nat hesitated.

"We're both wondering about Jeff," Felicity continued. "I mean, he's very handsome, and he looks like Bill, and . . ."

Carm burst out laughing. "And I just met him this morning. You two romantic fools! This is not a Hallmark movie. If Jeff's interested, which I doubt, he knows where I live, or at least he can find out. Now, begone!"

Sheepishly, Nat and Felicity left the room, but then stopped and stared at each other. "Do you believe her?" Nat asked.

Felicity shook her head. "Methinks the lady protests too much."

"Definitely," Nat said.

Or, Felicity reflected, Carm finds it more comfortable to yearn for the impossible, something requiring no action on her part.

They returned to the living room and met Peter, who would drive them back to the camper for their last night there.

———◆———

In some ways, I'll miss our little home on wheels, Felicity thought, as she packed the rest of her belongings. Peter would pick up her bags and boxes in the morning and store them at the new house. She would take very little on the plane. Nat had completed her packing, including a small bag of basics for Joey, and then had fallen asleep. She'd had next to no sleep the night before.

What an amazing day, going from fear, loneliness, and no plans, all the way to reuniting with Carm, buying a house, acquiring a housemate with pet, and finally earning Peter's trust. He knows so much, he simply must be the Griffon, she thought. He's every bit as mysterious as LaSalle's lost ship—appearing and disappearing, sometimes as a vision in the fog. She had learned more as they sat on a bench outside of Water's Edge. Peter refused to say much in the car. "You can never be sure," he'd said. About bugging, she supposed he meant. The air had felt as if it would snow any second, but she'd sat close to Peter and pretended to be toasty warm.

Felicity hoped Peter was right about not telling Carm about Mrs. Usher. After all, their paths could cross in Aurora. Peter felt Carm would be safer not knowing, though, and Felicity would respect his wishes. "We still don't know everything about her, ourselves, or exactly what led her to Washington Island and the daycare center. Helen's husband was involved somehow. We'll continue to stay alert." Felicity was relieved to learn that Helen had been taken to a safe house, somewhere along the border of Minnesota and Manitoba.

Mrs. Usher and her husband were dangerous, Peter had said, because they had power and were stupid. "A terrible combination, and they've been swayed by a tragedy that would affect anyone."

Felicity learned that the Ushers' son was an ICE agent, murdered by an illegal immigrant. "Mrs. Usher has decided the murderer was from Ecuador, like Joey. Actually, he escaped from Argentina, and some might find the murder justified. But people like the Ushers dump all immigrants into one basket, no matter the circumstances or what country they're from."

That explained some of Mrs. Usher's bizarre behavior at the hospital. Felicity almost felt sorry for her.

Possibly the most shocking thing Peter told her was that they'd identified the leak at the hospital—the reason the Code Pink operation ended. "A nurse named Becky," Peter said. "She didn't kill Selena but definitely reported her to those who did."

Felicity remembered the gloomy, unpleasant nurse, who did not match her perky name. How could a nurse be involved in such hatred and violence?

"Becky, if that's her name, worked at other hospitals where we had Code Pink operations: Code Pink drills on a Saturday, and then the actual movements of immigrants the next day when the staff was lighter and more relaxed. Unfortunately, the nurse recognized Selena. Babies who were part of our Code Pink operation were in pretty bad shape when they arrived at our hospitals. Joey was malnourished and had a severe flesh wound. Doctors and nurses dealt with the babies' needs and didn't ask questions. But later, the questions came, and it was time to get moving."

Felicity had shivered, from the plight of the poor babies as well as the temperature.

"Felicity, you're freezing. We've been sitting here far too long."

"One more thing, Peter, if you can tell me. All of the children are important, of course, but why is there so much fuss about Joey? Why did he and his mother leave Ecuador? I thought that was a fairly stable country."

But Peter didn't answer. "Maybe another time, Felicity. I don't know for certain. What is certain, though, is that both of us are cold."

And tired, too, Felicity thought as she closed the last bag. She should try to sleep. Peter would take them to the airport at 5:00 a.m. — she looked at the wall clock — in only a few more hours.

CHAPTER NINETEEN

CARM JOINED ASTRID IN THE kitchen for a late breakfast. That is, breakfast for Carm. Astrid had eaten hours before but was finishing the dishes. Only a few guests were staying at the inn, although they were fully booked for Thanksgiving, less than two weeks away.

"I guess they got off okay," Carm said. "I meant to say goodbye, at least to Jeff, but I couldn't talk myself out of bed."

Astrid laughed. "After what you've been through, I don't wonder. Well, Peter reported that the plane took off before the sun came up, so they're probably fine. I hope the weather won't be a problem. It's snowing heavily in northern Minnesota. Fortunately, I was able to lend Felicity a warm jacket and boots. Mike found clothing for Nat and Joey at the daycare center. You don't have adequate clothing for this time of year, either."

"It was still early fall when we left home. I'm sorry I missed them. What about Jeff?"

"You only missed him by an hour. He left his car keys and said he'd call you."

Carm took a long sip of coffee, and then sighed. "Still such a long way to go."

"More?" Astrid filled her cup. "You seem anxious to be home."

"I can't wait, but I don't think Flick and Nat understand."

"Maybe because neither consider it home."

Carm shook her head. "It isn't Nat's, of course, but Flick has lived in Aurora her whole life."

"Without ever feeling at home."

"She will be happier here," Carm admitted, "but I'll miss her." She would, of course, but it might be a relief not worrying about her. She felt guilty for even thinking such a thing. And she felt even guiltier about Nat, who truly was her responsibility. But no, she did not want to live with a teenage girl and a dog in the townhouse she did not want to leave.

"Felicity will make fine company for me," Astrid said. "Such an interesting, intelligent woman! And I hope you'll visit often. Now I'd best dust the furniture. We've got people going and people coming. Just the way I like it."

"Thanks for everything, Astrid." When she left the room, Carm shook her head. Was Flick smart, or at least smart enough for someone to notice? She'd only attended junior college. True, she read a lot and did the *Times* crossword puzzle quickly, without stopping for breath. So maybe Flick was smart. Carm had always found her needy.

"Now what?" she whispered. What might she do for the rest of the day? She wanted to call Bill, but it would be safer for Jeff to do it. She could try to get in touch with Nat's stepmother, Katy, and a lawyer. Carm would become Nat's legal guardian and learn what Nat's rights were. She did not believe her brother would have left his daughter destitute. Perhaps she and Flick could share custody. Yes, she'd get to work and try to make things pleasant for everyone.

———◆———

"The snow is getting worse," Nat said from the backseat of the Cessna Skyhawk. "I don't know how you can see where we're going." She held Joey, who was sound asleep because of the movement and endless humming of the engine. Aunt Flick was also asleep, seated in the front seat next to pilot Mike. Before Peter had picked them up at the camper, she had admitted to Nat that she had been awake all night. It seemed strange not hearing Flick's input.

"Barely seeing," Mike said. "Fortunately, I've been in this area before. Actually, I'm less worried about the snow than I am the radio. We seem to have lost contact with the ground."

Nat noticed that his hands were white from gripping the wheel so tightly, and his voice was tight. Mike wasn't just worried; he was scared. "What are you going to do?"

"Land, I'm afraid. Without being able to make contact, I can't at an airport. I'd planned to find out which one is the safest place to cross today—Pine Creek Border or Warroad. I'd prefer Pine Creek, but neither looks promising at the moment."

"Land where?"

"With any luck, near a family I know. Now, I really must concentrate."

In other words, stop talking. Mike would have an easier time if old, young, and in-between passengers remained silent.

Nat stared out the window, trying to find anything she could identify. It was still morning, but it might as well be night. The world out there was a gigantic snow globe without objects—just a violent swirl of white flakes.

And this was to be her world. From Las Cruces, New Mexico, where she had no memory of snow ever falling, to a white wonderland. There would be plenty of snow in Washington Island, for at least some of the year. Would she like that? She felt herself growing anxious. Relax, she thought. Joey might feel your nervousness and wake up.

Think about something besides the storm, she told herself firmly. Not Dad—that hurts too much—or Katy. Being hurt or angry would cause her to tense up again. Flick's new house and having an apartment in it was a lovely topic. Nat was certain to inherit money from Dad. She'd use some to decorate. She had a few pieces of furniture in Las Cruces that she could ship to the island. True, she was a little apprehensive about a new school, but with so few students, she was bound to receive individual help. It wouldn't matter so much that she was far behind. And she would be with Flick, daycare center friends — and Mike.

"Hold on to your hats," he said suddenly. "Down we go!"

Nat put on a brave face. "I'll hold on to the baby," she said.

CHAPTER TWENTY

IT WAS A HARD LANDING, and Felicity woke with a start. "Oh, are we there already? Did I sleep through the whole trip?"

Oddly, Joey remained asleep, perhaps because Nat continued rocking him. "Not quite," she said. "Take a look out the window."

"At what?" Felicity said, somewhat sharpish. She'd been having a pleasant dream about choosing items for her new house and throwing away everything she didn't like. It would be a first for her. She looked out the window. "Nothing out there but snow."

"Exactly," Nat said. "Don't talk so loud. I want Joey to sleep a little longer."

"Emergency landing," Mike explained. "The storm made it hard to see, of course, but the main problem is the radio isn't working. I can't land at an airport without instructions. You three stay here, and I'll go find help. I have friends, who live somewhere around here." Mike pulled on his gloves and took a flashlight from a pocket of his heavy jacket. "If you're cold, blankets are on the floor next to you, Nat. I'll be back as soon as I can."

"Wait a minute! Can't we go with you?"

Mike shook his head. "I'll make better time alone, and you aren't wearing the right clothing. Don't worry. You'll be safe here."

And then, after seeing Mike disappear into a cluster of tall trees, they were alone. Nat held a finger to her lips as a warning to keep still, but she could tell what Flick was thinking. Could they be sure of Mike? "He would never abandon his plane," she whispered, and started humming Joey's favorite bedtime song.

Felicity nodded, although she wasn't certain what to believe. But if Mike intended to kill them, he wouldn't have chosen this unlikely method. Leave them to starve or freeze to death? There were plenty of faster and surer options. If only she and Nat could talk, but then, who knew how long they'd have to keep Joey amused? At least silence wasn't such a problem anymore. No Ralph to whip himself into a sudden rage before grabbing his belt. Some scars remained, though, as reminders.

She should use this time to think, not worry. Soon, possibly today, they would turn Joey over to friendly hands. They would say goodbye to someone they loved and would never see again. Would they ever learn his story? Peter had told her an Argentinian immigrant had killed Mrs. Usher's son. What did she know about Argentina? Not much, despite seeing *Evita* three times at the Paramount. Don't cry for me, Argentina, she hummed in her head. Never mind, Evita. Better to cry for an Argentina that needs all the tears it can get.

But Joey came from Ecuador, not Argentina, even though Mrs. Usher put all South American countries into one basket. Felicity didn't think she knew anything about Ecuador, except it was a democracy. She had read recently that violent crime was a problem. What else had she read? In the *Trib*, there was a story about a lawyer the government considered a darned nuisance. The lawyer—what was his name? Something Garcia—was organizing demonstrations to protest attacks on journalists, civil rights organizations, and the government's excessive use of force. The article mentioned that Garcia's wife and baby son appeared to be missing. Garcia insisted they were just on an extended holiday.

What if that son were Joey? What if his father had arranged for the mother and son to get over the border, but somehow they were separated? Felicity knew that Joey had been malnourished and wounded. Could some extremist group have offered a bounty on him, thinking that if he were captured, his father would fall into line?

Garcia's wife had a weird name. Now, what was it? Aaronisha Maria, that was it! Felicity shrugged. What were her parents thinking? It was unlikely that the Garcias were Joey's parents, but it was possible. She pulled a small flashlight from her bag and held it tightly. Somehow it offered protection from her grim thoughts and the menacing outdoors.

◆

Nat felt a stirring in her arms. Oh, well, she was lucky he had slept as long as he had. "Na-lee?"

"Natalie is here, honey. So is Flick."

"Ffff . . ." Joey's efforts to say Flick were always amusing.

"We're in the airplane, Joey, waiting for Mike." He wouldn't understand airplane, but he did know Mike.

Joey looked around and frowned. His lower lip quivered. Please don't cry, Joey, Nat pleaded inwardly. When Joey let loose, it was almost impossible to soothe him. His storm would be as great as the real one outside. "Snow, snow, snow," Nat started singing tunelessly. "Help me, Aunt Flick."

Felicity got into the spirit. "Snow, snow, snow, see it blow, see it go, all for Jo—ey."

Joey changed his mind about crying and giggled in delight. But the happy mood would not last long, Nat knew. He needed his diaper changed, and he was bound to be hungry soon. "Aunt Flick, how long has Mike been gone?"

Using the flashlight, Felicity examined her watch. "Just over an hour," she said. "Seems longer."

"Too long. I'm scared. I'm sure he planned on coming right back, but what if something happened to him? Should I go look?"

Felicity shook her head. "Look where? He seemed to have a destination in mind. No, we have to wait longer. But I really wish I could go to the bathroom."

Nat groaned. "Don't mention it."

As hard as it was, they played peek-a-boo, the itsy bitsy spider, and sang every silly song they knew. And they hoped and prayed, trying to ignore that they were alone and enclosed in a dark, aluminum shell, where they were getting colder and colder.

Finally, Joey had enough of their nonsense. "Car!" he yelled.

"No, darling, Carm isn't here." Felicity almost said that he'd see her soon, but stopped. Joey would never see Carm again. She only hoped she and Nat would.

"Car!" Joey yelled again. Felicity started another song to distract him.

"Wait, Aunt Flick. Listen. This time, I don't think he means Carm. It's Mike, in a car!"

Thank goodness! Felicity could just make it out. "Not a car," she said. "It's a snowmobile. Only room for one passenger, though."

Mike, looking like an exhausted snowman, opened the pilot's door. "Sorry it took so long," he said. "Knew you'd be worried. I became disoriented but finally found the safe house. They're looking for a vehicle we can use for the rest of the trip."

"But what about now?" Nat asked impatiently. "The snow has let up some. Can't you try the plane again?"

Mike shook his head. "Too risky without a radio. I was able to reach Peter. He said not to fly until the plane has been checked thoroughly. Just in case—" He stopped.

Just in case the radio was tampered with at the airport in Washington Island, Felicity thought. A whole new packet of troubles to think about later. It was unlikely the Ushers had anything to do with the airplane, although she might have preferred them as the culprits. At least those enemies had faces. It was the invisible ones that were scary. "You can only take one passenger," she observed.

"Yes," Mike agreed. "I'll take one of you holding Joey, and then I'll come back for the other. I'm sorry, but even a four-wheeler couldn't get through this mess. Now, who is going with me? It should take about thirty minutes each way."

Silence while the women considered how to nominate the other. Finally, "Flick should go," Nat said. "Aunt Flick, I know you're going to say it should be me, but face it. You're much older and haven't been out of the hospital that long. Aunt Carm said you almost died."

Felicity wanted to protest. After all, she was the adult; Nat was the child. But Nat was right. Felicity's body couldn't handle much more today. She was old, she was cold, and she needed a bathroom, even more than Joey needed a new diaper. "Okay," she said quietly. "Mike, help me out, and then give me Joey. Nat, pack a few essentials for him. Then while we're gone, consolidate just a few things we might need for the rest of the trip. You won't be able to take everything."

Nat nodded but didn't say anything. There was no good solution. Flick gave her a quick hug and handed her the precious flashlight. Then it happened quickly. They were gone.

—◆—

Had she ever been so alone in her life? Had she ever been so scared? Well, yes, when she knew her father was dead and that she and Al had to make their slow journey by train to Aurora. In some ways that was worse, for she truly had been abandoned. This was different. She was physically alone, and the fright came from the elements, not from people's indifference. Sure, Mike and Aunt Flick meant to return, but what if they couldn't? What if something happened to them? Would she just stay here and starve—and freeze?

"Daddy!" Nat hadn't called him that since she was eight. Now, finally, she began to cry. "How could you leave me? I know you loved me!" But he had been so sick. At the end, he hardly knew what he was doing or saying. It was his choice to end his life in Switzerland, but had it been his decision to leave her? Katy definitely wanted her out of the picture. "Daddy, I miss you!"

Stop right now! She scolded herself. The end result would have been the same. He was going to die. You and he did fine together, until Katy came along. But could you have helped him as Katy had?

Probably not. Suddenly, she was anxious to go with Aunt Carm to New Mexico. Daddy must have left a will providing for her with the lawyer. He wouldn't just desert her. He just wasn't well enough at the end to make decisions. Maybe someday, she and Aunt Flick could go to Switzerland and visit the town where Daddy had died. Meanwhile, she was young and strong and would be fine. "If I don't end up scaring myself to death."

Nat turned on the flashlight and examined the items in Flick's large bag. Three granola bars! Excellent! She'd eat them right now. Diapers and baby food, of course, money and phones, and—really, Flick—a book? *The Scarlet Pimpernel*, the one Aunt Flick had borrowed from Water's Edge with a character that reminded Flick of Peter. Nat turned a blanket into a tent, as she had when she was a little girl, and began reading, hoping it would make the time fly.

But time didn't fly—it crawled. Hours passed. The book was good, when she could concentrate. She could see why Aunt Flick had chosen one about brave people rescuing those in trouble, helping them escape to another country. In some ways, it was like right now.

The flashlight grew weaker and weaker, and then failed. Whimpering, Nat withdrew completely under the blanket. Finally, she slept.

———◆———

Carm sat in the kitchen, mindlessly eating pastries and drinking cup after cup of strong, black coffee. It would be amazing if she slept that night. Astrid had spent as much time as she could afford talking with her, but beds needed to be stripped and made, and tonight's dinner prepared. Carm felt useless and very much alone. But earlier, although she had not been able to contact Katy, she had reached her brother's lawyer, who assured her that Nat's financial needs had been addressed in her father's will. There was little for Katy, who seemed to have disappeared. The lawyer, a Mr. Benson, would meet with her when she and Nat arrived. "Tomorrow or the next day," Carm told Mr. Benson, although she had no way of knowing for sure.

She wished she could grieve for Charles, really grieve, and not just say the right words to others. But she had never really known him. Years older, he moved from Illinois as soon as he could afford to get away from their parents, who were loving toward each other but no one else. They did their custodial duty to their children but spared them much affection. Flick hadn't received love, either. In fact, quite the opposite, but she gave it, along with kindness, to everyone. How was that possible? What made people positive and resilient when they had no reason to be? Now, finally, with Ralph behind her, Flick would make friends wherever she went, while she, Carm, had acquaintances, but only two friends—Bill and Flick, who would no longer be with her. Flick—whom Carm had never appreciated the way she should.

The back door opened suddenly, and Peter walked into the room. "Got any coffee?" he asked. "Cold out there."

Carm poured him a cup, and watched as he added an unusual amount of cream and sugar. "Have you heard anything?"

"Just a second." He took a long sip. "Yes, just got some news. I'm afraid it might be a few days before you can start south with Natalie. A heavy snow has grounded the plane. They're going to have to drive the rest of the way."

"How?"

"They landed near a place that Mike knows, where he will borrow a four-wheel drive. That part will be okay, but they won't be able to fly the plane back here. We haven't figured out the rest of the trip yet."

"But the snow may let up."

Peter shook his head. "Something's off with the radio. Can't take a chance until the plane is inspected. I don't know—"

He thinks someone might have sabotaged it, Carm thought. What a world these people live in! "So I guess I'll keep on eating too many of your sister's desserts and drinking too much coffee—and wait."

Peter smiled. "I can think of worse things to do, but I thought you might like a tour of the island and Felicity's new house. I could use some distraction, too."

"Just a sec. Astrid lent me a coat," Carm said.

CHAPTER TWENTY-ONE

I APPRECIATE YOUR DOING THIS, Peter," Carm said, "but I'll admit I'm surprised. I didn't think you liked me very much."

Peter shrugged. "Well, I didn't, but Felicity said you probably saved her life and that you're the best friend she's ever had. I decided I should know you better."

"She's the best friend I've ever had, too. Neither of us has been lucky in the friend department. Me, because I'm, well, me. My own fault. But in different circumstances, Flick would have been the most popular person anywhere she went. But—" Nat paused.

"Her husband abused her."

"Horribly, and so did her father. Her mother never stood up for her, and then died young. Probably to get away from her husband."

"But Felicity's husband must have loved her at first."

Carm shook her head. "No, Ralph only pretended at first. Actually, he bought her?"

"What?"

"Call it a business arrangement between her father and Ralph. Flick was not loved. And it wasn't even a classic abuse situation. Ralph never apologized or even felt he was wrong. He was just angry all the time. Until—" Carm told Peter how she'd met Felicity and how Ralph had died. "It's taken Flick a long time to find herself. It's amazing how much she's changed on this trip alone."

"She's a miracle," Peter said. "After all she's been through, to still enjoy life and see the good in everyone. And be, well, lovable."

Why, he's in love with her, or on the brink of falling. Carm watched him turn his back to hide his blush. She wondered if Flick had any idea. Well, if anyone deserved happiness, Flick did. The hard part for Peter, of course, would be to convince Flick that anyone could love her. For the first time, Carm wondered if she would be lonely, back in Aurora.

Perhaps Peter picked up on her thoughts. "You can come for a visit any time you want," he said. "Felicity will have plenty of room."

And the house was everything Flick had said it was. Roomy, a perfect location, and it seemed to have a definite personality, happy, not the gloom and despair of Ralph's house, which had never belonged to Flick. The furnishings were so-so, but Flick and Nat would enjoy redecorating, without money being a problem. "I shall insist on a special guest room," Carm said.

On the way back to the inn, Carm asked Peter how Washington Island got its name. "It seems such an odd choice," she said. "Most of the longtime residents are descended from Iceland settlers. Shouldn't it be called Jorgenson Island, or something like that?"

"You have a point," Peter agreed, "especially since that's my last name. It's the second oldest Icelandic settlement in the country. But Washington Island is named after a ship of that name that came here in 1816. Its sailors' mission was to prevent the English from turning the Indians against the settlers. The sailors had a rough time of it and gave the community the name, Washington, to honor the ship and the harbor that had sheltered them."

Carm shrugged. The name must be as confusing to others as it was to her. But she hadn't been around in 1816 to give her opinion.

Peter's phone gave a chirp. "Ah, word from our travelers," he said, checking the text. "Felicity and the baby are in safe hands, and Mike is returning to the plane for Natalie. By late tonight, little Joey should be with his mother."

"Good." Carm nodded. "Let's go back now. I should call Jeff, and there's no cell service here."

———◆———

"Nat," called a worried voice, "are you there? Why is it so dark?" He turned on his flashlight and reached into the back seat, poking at the form under the blanket.

"Hey! Who's there? Why are you shining that light in my eyes?" Nat pulled herself together. "Oh, it's you, Mike. Why didn't you say so?"

"I'm really sorry, Nat. It took much longer than I expected, but why aren't you using Flick's little flashlight?"

"I was reading a book, and the battery wore out. But can we just go?"

"Did you pack a bag?" Nat handed it to him. "Then let me help you out. If you've been crunched up like that for hours; you must be horribly stiff."

Nat let him guide her into the snowmobile. She could hardly think, much less talk. Her brain and heart were still in revolutionary France, trying to help Marguerite find her husband before being captured by his enemies. Aunt Flick's book had kept her sane, or at least from worrying about Flick, Joey, Mike—or herself. "You were gone hours!"

"I know," he soothed. "But it's over. You'll be all right now."

———◆———

Other than being worried about Nat, Felicity was having a grand time at the safe house run by a friend of Mike's older sister. Inez was as friendly as Felicity and happy to have a female visitor for a bit of gossip. What a difference being warm and full and having access to a bathroom made. She'd be quite content to stay here for a few days, if it weren't for Nat. It had taken Mike and Inez's husband too long to arrange for a car to take them the rest of the way and to figure out how they'd get home again. Nat must be beside herself, but at last Mike was on his way. She wouldn't have time to recover, though. Mike said they had to leave immediately. They wouldn't get to their next station until after dark, and then, if they determined it was safe,

Joey would cross the border into Manitoba. Felicity had no idea who would take him.

Joey, too, was having a wonderful time, playing with Inez's four-year-old daughter, Jenny, and her puppy. The two children laughed and giggled, and the puppy yipped. They seemed to be having an odd game, with the puppy clearly in charge. What a strange situation for a family, living a secret life in this small community of Deer River, population 909. Mike's plane had landed in the Chippewa National Forest. They were lucky, Inez said, to have found a flat place that was dry in an area that consisted largely of wetlands. The snow had actually made it easier to leave.

Finally, Nat arrived, and after receiving a hot meal as well as hugs from Aunt Flick and Joey, they were on their way in a sturdy Ford Bronco, brought up from Minneapolis by a man named Ted, who seemed unduly boisterous and full of chatter, considering the circumstances. "We have a whole fleet of cars to carry people to freedom. Yes," he boasted, "in Minnesota, we know how to do things! Our drivers take their lives in their hands every single day."

And other people's lives, too, Felicity thought, wondering how dangerous this trip would be for them. Ted said he would wait until they returned, and then they would go with him to Minneapolis, where they'd take a plane home. Felicity wasn't sure where they'd land but knew they'd find out at some point.

"I'll tell you more in the car," Mike promised. It would take them over three hours to get to Pine Creek, near the Manitoba border. "It's farm country; not much there. I wasn't sure whether Warroad would be safer—it varies—but Inez's husband assures me that tonight, at least, Piney/Pinecreek is the best bet. It's smaller and much more remote."

"I like Inez," Felicity said. "I'm glad I'll get to see her again."

"Yes, although we won't stay long. I'm sure Ted will need to return quickly to Minneapolis. For all of his bragging, he's one of the bravest men I know."

"Then we'll get a plane in Minneapolis, but what about your plane?" Nat, in the back seat, was cuddling Joey, who had fallen asleep again.

"Ted and some trusted mechanics will go over it, and then someone will fly it back to Washington Island, as soon as—"

"As soon as they're sure no one back home has tinkered with the radio," Felicity said.

Mike grinned. "You don't miss much, do you, Flick? I'd better concentrate on the road before you get anything more out of me."

"One more thing," Nat said, "and then I'll shut up." Weird thing to say, considering all the hours she'd said nothing. "Where will our Minneapolis flight end? Where are we going?"

"Milwaukee, and then we'll rent a car, although I won't be surprised if Peter meets us. He's been kind of anxious—for him, anyway."

"The Scarlet Pimpernel," Nat muttered, before joining Joey in sleep.

Felicity, overhearing, smiled, and then closed her eyes until—

A siren, sounding as if it were on top of them, jarred them awake. Mike pulled to the side of the road, clearly shaken. "Quick. We need a cover story. Why are we here?"

"You've got all the papers for this car, right?" Felicity asked. Mike nodded, pointing to the glove box. "Well, we aren't doing anything wrong. Let's just say that you're my grandchildren and Joey is my great-grandson. We've been visiting my husband at the hospital in . . ."

"Crookston," Nat offered. "I saw the sign."

"Good. And we're going home to . . ."

"Warren," Mike said. "I saw it on the map. Going there sort of makes sense, I guess. Well, it's almost here."

Then they saw what was making the racket, and they burst out laughing. There were two—a fire engine and an ambulance, speeding past the Bronco. Felicity gave a silent prayer for the people who needed help, and then she relaxed, ready to forget the whole thing.

But Nat wasn't. "Why were you so scared, Mike? You've done things like this lots of times."

Mike's voice shook. "Never before in a car, thinking people were trying to stop us. Me, I usually fly to a border airport, and then let other people take over. I really thought we were done for. I'll be all right in a second. Please don't tell—"

Peter, Felicity thought he must mean. "Don't worry, Mike. This has been a stressful trip for everyone, especially you."

Nat nodded. "Walking for hours in that forest, not knowing if you'd find help—I can't imagine it!" Then Joey saved them from further embarrassment by waking up and demanding attention.

An hour and a half later, they arrived at their destination, a small cabin. A blue Honda, sporting Canadian license plates, parked outside. Inside were a man and woman ready to leave. They were pleasant enough, but business-like and in a hurry. Without asking permission, the woman gave Joey a spoonful of something.

"No," Nat protested.

"It's all right," the woman said. "Please don't worry. It won't harm him, but it is essential that he sleep, and my guess is that he's been sleeping too much since your trip began."

"But he always sleeps on car rides." Felicity didn't like the idea of drugging Joey, either.

"We can't take a chance." The woman smiled. "Now say your goodbyes. We must go quickly. I'll be back tomorrow morning to report how things went."

Felicity gave Joey a kiss and a hug. She had no words.

Natalie hugged Joey until the woman cleared her throat. Finally— "Bye, bye, Joey. I love you."

Joey touched her face. "Na-lee, bye, bye." Natalie handed him to the woman, and they were gone.

Felicity held out her arms, and Natalie rushed into them. They sobbed until there were no tears left.

"Let's vow right now to always help children in trouble. It will be our mission."

"Yes," Nat agreed.

◆

The woman was there when Felicity and Nat awoke early the next morning. "See, I kept my promise," she said. "No need to worry. All is well. This is for you from Jorge's Mama." She gave Felicity a note and left the cabin.

"It's in Spanish. Please translate it."

Nat examined the fancy cursive that made the Spanish even harder to read. Okay, but I may need help figuring out some of the letters." Finally —

To the ladies who saved Jorge.

"So, his name is really Georgie. We were close."

"Go on, Nat."

Nat continued haltingly.

My dear husband and I will think of you with gratitude our entire lives. Jorge seems to know who I am, although it is not surprising he is bewildered by all the changes. Soon we will celebrate his first birthday. I will see that he remembers you. If your country continues down its present path, perhaps he will rescue you someday.

Quite a dig, Felicity thought, but she really couldn't blame the poor woman. She must have been frantic about her baby, as well as dismayed at the country that separated them. "Was it signed?"

"Yes. Just initials, though. She says: *Forever your friend, A.M.G.*"

Aaronisha Maria Garcia, Felicity thought. It could be. Maybe I was right. "She mentioned her husband. Perhaps he's there or will be soon."

Nat returned the note. "Jorge. I'll always think of him as Joey. We'll miss him, Aunt Flick."

"But at least he's safe." Felicity sat in an over-stuffed chair and looked out at a bleak Canadian landscape. It was still snowing but was supposed to taper off before noon.

Nat cuddled up on a couch near the fireplace to continue reading *The Scarlet Pimpernel.* She understood why the French Revolution started and why the people were angry. But then it got entirely out of hand, and a small group of people tried to make it right by saving lives. That's what was happening here, in a way. Immigration was a huge problem, for the people trying to escape horrible conditions, as well as those overwhelmed and no longer able or willing to help. She shrugged. She supposed she was simplifying it too much, but she was trying to understand. Many people, such as Mike, Peter, Astrid, and Josephina, were trying to keep children like Joey safe. Others like Selena and Trey had died trying. Some they'd met on their trip were nameless, or using false names, such as the woman they met in Hebron their first night. But they all had played their parts and had stories.

"We have stories, too, Aunt Flick."

Felicity nodded, seeming to understand the thoughts behind Nat's words.

"I love this book, Aunt Flick."

———◆———

Felicity's phone chirped. Service at last! And her first secret text message!

> **URR:**
> **The Griffon to The Phoenix**
> **Delete after reading**
> **Thank goodness you're safe!**
> **Mission successful. Well done!**
> **Your home and I are waiting.**
> **My love, P.T.R.**

Peter the Rock—and also the Griffon. Felicity had been right all along. And she was the Phoenix, rising, reinventing herself. Before following directions by deleting the text, she read the last line again. Her face burned with embarrassment. If Nat noticed, Felicity would blame the fire.

Your love, Peter? Well, we'll see—we'll wait and see.

About the Author

CODE PINK is Marilyn's twelfth novel. Some years back, she was in the hospital, with a similar condition as her character, when a Code Pink drill took place. Like Felicity, she had no idea what that meant. Intrigued, she wrote the words in her journal and vowed to find out more. This experience, plus a growing attachment to Washington Island, resulted in *Code Pink*.

Marilyn lives in Downers Grove, Illinois with her husband Ed and cat Dinah. She is a theater director and lifetime member of the Downers Grove Historical Society.

Gratitude always to Ellie Searl, for her skill, artistry, and enduring friendship.